BOOST BRAIN POWER

52 Ways to Use What Science Tells Us

Jill Stamm, PhD

Gryphon House
www.gryphonhouse.com

Published by Gryphon House, Inc.
P. O. Box 10, Lewisville, NC 27023
800.638.0928; 877.638.7576 (fax)
Visit us on the web at www.gryphonhouse.com.

Bulk Purchase

Gryphon House books are available for special premiums and sales promotions as well as for fund-raising use. Special editions or book excerpts also can be created to specifications. For details, call 800.638.0928.

Disclaimer

Gryphon House Inc. cannot be held responsible for damage, mishap, or injury incurred during the use of or because of activities in this book. Appropriate and reasonable caution and adult supervision of children involved in activities and corresponding to the age and capability of each child involved are recommended at all times. Do not leave children unattended at any time. Observe safety and caution at all times.

Library of Congress Cataloging-in-Publication Data
Names: Stamm, Jill, author.
Title: Boosting brain power : 52 ways to use what science tells us / Jill
    Stamm.
Description: Lewisville, NC : Gryphon House, Inc., [2016] | Includes
    bibliographical references and index.
Identifiers: LCCN 2015041303 | ISBN 9780876593592
Subjects: LCSH: Cognition in children. | Thought and thinking. | Brain. |
    Intellect.
Classification: LCC BF723.C5 S73 2016 | DDC 155.42/33--dc23 LC record available
at http://lccn.loc.gov/2015041303

This book is dedicated to my daughters,

Jenny and Kristin

Acknowledgments

There are several people I want to thank for helping me to write this book. I have worked with a group of people at Arizona's Children Association and specifically with adjunct faculty and staff at New Directions Institute for Infant Brain Development, who helped me to refine and distill the often complex ideas from neuroscientists and researchers into simple, concrete messages. They have challenged me to make my ideas shorter, yet very clear. Because nearly all people in the United States have more data bombarding them than ever before in history, it is important to try to communicate efficiently in formats that busy people can absorb. Thank you.

I also want to thank my daughter Kristin Stamm McNealy. This delightful girl grew up to become a highly educated neuroscientist. It is just wonderful to have my very own little neuroscientist in my pocket whom I can call up to discuss important questions that, as an educator, I have needed help to understand. Not only do we have amazing times learning from each other, but she has also been my editor and colleague in this current book, my previous *Bright from the Start* book, our *Brain Boxes® Education Systems*, and other projects I have been working on. Bless you, Kristin.

And I am always grateful to my daughter Jenny for showing me every day that, even with special needs and against all odds, each person can make a profound difference in this world. Jenny has been, and remains, my supreme teacher.

Contents

Part 4: Attention Messages

Part 5: Bonding Messages

Part 6: Communication Messages

INTRODUCTION

What Caregivers Can Easily Learn about Brain Development

In the desire to help our youngest children develop strong, healthy minds and important qualities of character and caring, we can start by thinking about how each of us will answer a common question, "*Why* does early childhood matter?"

I am asked this question often. I am asked to define, "What specifically has been discovered that requires a change in the kind of care young children receive?" Some of the new information comes from neuroscientists who detail how to protect a developing brain; some has been reported by economists who calculate cost savings resulting from improved early care and education for young children. Other new information is derived from longitudinal studies that link the quality of childhood experiences to long-term health outcomes.

This book is designed to help caregivers use new knowledge that has been created by a variety of sources. Anyone caring for young children has questions about everyday concerns. These questions deserve simple but accurate answers. This book provides caregivers—including center-based staff, in-home family child care providers, nannies, early childhood–education students, parents, and other family members—with easy-to-understand messages that translate complex science-based information about early brain development into simple actions you can take to encourage healthy development in infants, toddlers, and preschoolers. Now that neuroscience has revealed such critical information about how brains actually develop, educators and caregivers can use these key ideas to implement a variety of new strategies and perspectives in their classrooms and child care settings.

This book provides short statements called "Brain Nuggets" that inform caregivers about the latest important information on early brain development. These are clustered into the categories of general science, attention, bonding, and communication. You might decide to skip some introductory information for now and go right to the first Brain Nugget. That is just fine. You can start and stop where you choose. Because there are fifty-two main ideas explained in the book, you could easily approach the content by reading and thinking about one idea each week of the year. I want to emphasize the notion of thinking about a main idea. Each person who cares for young children has a different story, a different reason she wants to help young children, and a different amount of formal education about child development. Because the science of early brain development is so new, caregivers also have different (and probably limited) amounts of formal instruction about the brain of a child. This book can guide your efforts to create environments and relationships that can make a difference, based on what researchers have learned about the social-emotional and intellectual development of young children.

For more than a decade, the general public has been exposed to reports detailing recent findings from neuroscience about how young brains develop. Yet only recently have leaders in government agencies, community organizations, and corporations committed to expecting educators to apply those findings to their practices and policies on caring for and educating children from birth to five years old. You can find a mountain of evidence revealing the factors that are known to have an impact on the trajectory of development, either healthy or challenged. The problem has been, and remains, that it can be difficult for the scientists who conduct and share study results to also offer clear, simple, and comprehensible applications of this important information. Their attempts may have missed the mark because either they are too technical and text laden, thereby making comprehension time consuming and demanding, or they provide only broad-sweeping summaries that lack enough detail for the reader to be able to know what to do with the information.

This book offers clear, succinct key findings from neuroscience to help teachers and caregivers understand some of what I call "Brain Basics 101," which in turn help when explaining why specific behaviors, environments, and practices can be so helpful in securing normal, healthy brain development. The book then offers prevention strategies that have been shown to be easily learned and implemented in care environments and classrooms for infants, toddlers, and preschoolers. The Brain Nuggets in this book offer simple, concrete ways of understanding why the quality of care matters so much to a developing brain. Anyone who cares for and loves a young child can benefit by knowing what the science shows. References to research are noted so that you can do further reading if you desire. But the main point is that easy-to-learn ideas, guides, and suggestions can help you be more deliberate in the interactions you have with young children. Quality care that is intentional matters. When caregivers understand why their role is so critical to the actual development of a child's brain, several things follow.

First, many caregivers will feel a novel sense of pride in their work. They can now see themselves as key figures in the lives of children. Even if they had hoped for this role, they often felt their contributions were not recognized. This increased sense of self-efficacy can benefit the overall field of early care. Because it is unlikely that early care–workforce wages will see a rapid increase in the near future, talented staff will more likely decide to continue in their current roles or perhaps seek additional education once they understand their true value to society.

Second, caregivers can start to create environments and activities on purpose, instead of by accident or by instinct. A growing body of scientific research on mindfulness explains why this development occurs. When you are *intentional*—meaning *mindful of your actions*—you can greatly increase the likelihood that you will take a desired action. From human behavior, we know that when you plan and understand why you want a certain outcome, you will naturally commit more fully to see that it happens. The quality of care given to children increases dramatically when teachers and caregivers understand the reasons they should take certain actions.

The educational mandates in most states now include an emphasis on school-readiness efforts and programs. In almost every incarnation, the school-readiness concept focuses on specific skills that a child should have before entering kindergarten. However, policy makers provide very little money or planning for accomplishing those goals. Although a mandate on meeting specific benchmarks is understandable, the policies seem to hinge on a general misunderstanding that school readiness can be achieved simply by expecting historically agreed-upon primary-grade skills to be demonstrated earlier and earlier among preschool children. Parents feel it. Preschool teachers feel it. Caregivers know it is coming. The *it* is the unrealistic expectation that caregivers, child care directors, early care providers, and education staff will somehow automatically know how to protect and manage early brain development! This kind of knowledge will not happen by magic. Nor will it occur by just creating lists of activities that promise to result in school readiness. The activities themselves are not the most important aspect of school readiness. Rather, a child needs a ready brain that is capable of learning the different skills parents, caregivers, and teachers present at appropriate times in the child's development.

How then can we think about school readiness from the perspective of a child's brain? For a child to learn, she needs to allocate her attention to a task long enough to learn the information. The child needs to develop enough impulse control to be able to inhibit her desire to shift her attention and instead to stay on task.

A child's ability to focus involves understanding that he is safe and feeling secure that people love him. He needs to feel bonded to others. When a child has loving first relationships, he can grow and widen his circle appropriately to include others.

The child also needs to hear lots and lots of language spoken directly to her using words that describe and label not only objects in the environment but also relationships with others and the feelings the child experiences. Children need to develop both receptive and expressive communication. Mindfully, intentionally interacting with young children, promoting language-rich environments, and providing primary experiences for their brains to absorb can help prepare children for the challenges of formal schooling.

Preschool teachers and early care providers can work on being mindful every day to think about how they are focusing on each of these three areas: attention, bonding, and communication. This book will present these important concepts in short, pithy nuggets of information that can be applied in a classroom or used to create policies that benefit young children. The format is designed with busy caregivers in mind.

Each of the fifty-two segments provides a chunk of information or an idea summarizing research on early brain development. Each item begins with a concise statement that captures the essence of a larger idea using easy-to-understand language. You can reflect on the concepts and then use your prior knowledge and experience to think of how you can apply the principles.

Following each concise statement is an explanation of why the information is important and how it can help caregivers. Each segment also provides suggestions for applying the information to different audiences. You may find strategies or various perspectives on how to begin modifying current environments and policies.

The information in this book has been field-tested in my work with thousands of early care and education staff members, caregivers, in-home providers, and families in Arizona for more than fifteen years. The organization I cofounded in 1998 to share early brain development information, New Directions Institute for Infant Brain Development, has taught these and related concepts in workshops to nearly 80,000 individuals.

PART 1
Brain Basics 101

To successfully interact with young children in ways that reflect current, well-informed understandings of the brain, you do not need to learn the formal name of every brain structure or to understand the workings of individual neurons, synapses, or neurotransmitters. However, you do need information about how a child's brain develops and what the brain needs to grow into a healthy, self-regulated, learning organ.

Thanks to imaging technologies, scientists can look inside a living person's brain and discover useful information for making a medical diagnosis. Researchers can also document in which specific brain regions the connections are emerging at various ages in a typically developing child. The ability to view the brain as a growing, changing organ has implications for anyone caring for a young child.

A child's brain develops in a predictable sequence. Knowing this sequence can help guide caregivers to choose which experiences to focus on and at what age. Caregivers should note that the timing of brain development matters because not all parts develop at the same time. Certain regions wire up rapidly, and other areas refine their connections over long periods of time.

How the Brain Develops

As you begin thinking of the brain's growth and development, it will help to know several basic ideas. The sequence of brain development occurs in four simultaneous, dynamic ways: back to front, inside to outside, bottom to top, and right to left.

Primarily, the brain has three component areas: the brain stem, the limbic system, and the neocortex.

As you learn and think about the structures and functions of a brain, a critical organizing principle is that the earlier in life a structure develops and connects, the more resistant it is to change. But change is not impossible. To be specific, some of the early developing areas in the back, inside, and bottom develop rapidly. Once these general regions wire up, they are harder to influence and change. Therefore, the brain stem, which is both inside and at the bottom of the brain, and the limbic system, which is in the very center of the inside, are more difficult to change. The neocortex is the outermost area and continues to develop and change throughout a person's life span.

To envision the sequence of the developing brain, examine the accompanying drawing of the brain regions. This sequence is described in more detail in the following section.

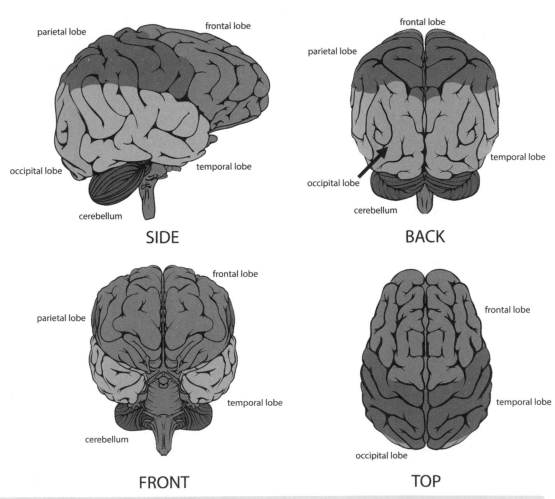

The Sequence

As noted, the brain develops in four simultaneous, predictable ways:

1. From the back to the front—The parts of the brain that process vision wire up first. Although babies cannot see clearly at birth, the wiring for normal sight occurs rapidly. By about six months, infants can see almost as well as many adults!

Then the hearing system wires up. Babies can hear in utero, and at birth, they can ... however, newborns cannot yet hear distinct ... small variations in sounds develops at a ... to learning the sounds of new languages ...

... the brain that bring together and combine ... sights and sounds wire up, allowing for ...

... are responsible for more complex thinking ... understanding the consequences of one's ... wiring up that continues to develop even ...

... s of the brain that will eventually connect ... emotions develop before the outer part, ... age of incoming information for thinking ... ure part of the limbic system, and the outer ...

... which is responsible for basic functions such ... re control, develops very early. Controlling ... linating fine motor movements are abilities ... .

4. From right to left—The right hemisphere is more active than the left hemisphere early in infancy. The left hemisphere begins to achieve its power as receptive and expressive language skills localize, or lateralize, into the left hemisphere during the end of the baby's first year. Recent research, as outlined by Martha Burns

on the website *Scientific Learning*, indicates that once skills are mastered, they tend to migrate to the left hemisphere. However, both hemispheres continue to communicate with each other throughout a person's lifetime. Functions that tend to remain associated with the right hemisphere include recognizing faces, reading emotions, processing language syntax and intonation, and demonstrating some music competencies.

This four-way progression is useful to know because it helps determine which skills young children usually learn at different times. This knowledge can help guide your choice of activities for children to engage in and help you understand why the timing of certain simple interactions is so important. Bonding is critical in the first year, for example, because the emotional centers of the brain develop so early. Therefore, if you are taking care of infants and young toddlers, pay close attention to the Brain Nuggets that are concerned with providing security and consistency for very young children. For children to achieve optimal development of more complex, later-developing systems, they will need to experience healthy development of the less complex, earlier-developing systems. Yes, scientists now know that the degree of safety and love a young child feels can directly affect the later development of other brain regions.

The Components

As you think about brain development, consider the functions of the three components: the brain stem, the limbic system, and the cortex.

- *Brain stem*—extending from the spinal cord and underneath the limbic system, this structure connects the spinal cord to the brain's regulatory areas that control basic life-sustaining operations such as breathing, heart rate, and temperature regulation. It is also involved in arousal and alertness.

- *Limbic system*—a collection of several structures that, when taken together, are responsible for processing incoming information and tagging it for its emotional importance, and for filing and retrieving memories. This brain region also plays a key role in motivation.

- *Cortex*—the outermost area of the brain consists of mostly gray matter that processes and stores information. The cortex is that folded, gray-colored image you likely picture when someone talks about the brain. The structures in this system work together to help someone pay attention, manage emotions, form and retrieve memories, make rational decisions, and carry out actions. The cortex has a remarkable ability to change, a quality called *plasticity*. At every age, the cortex is capable of learning and therefore changing with new input.

Although the cortex appears thin (the name means *outer bark*), it is actually six layers thick, with each layer serving a different function. The cortex consists of a great number of neurons, and it stores most of the information you learned in school, such as your memory for reading, math, science, and social studies, and your first and second languages.

The Timing and Influence

The most important thing that a teacher, caregiver, or parent needs to know about these brain regions is that the first two, the brain stem and the limbic system, form almost completely in the first five years of life! Yes, that is when early caregivers are in charge! If you recognize the importance of timing and understand the resistance of early developing areas to change later on, then you can clearly see that learning about the brain can help you provide high-quality, personal, loving care to a child. As care providers and teachers, you have a relatively easy job of dispensing information that will be stored in the later-developing neocortex. However, if you want to influence a child's emotional center and memory capabilities in the limbic system, then earlier is better. The infant, toddler, and preschool years are when you will have the greatest impact. You, as the caregiver, are working with children in prime time, and you have tremendous power to help develop a child's brain. So the next time a casual acquaintance learns that you work with young children and says, "Oh, so you are a babysitter," you can politely correct that notion and proudly answer, "No, actually, what I do for a living is help form children's brains!"

Brain Structure and Function

Because you have such a key role in fostering brain development, you have motivation to learn just enough about brain structure and function to do your job well. The diagrams of the brain included here, with various parts labeled, will give you reference points for information that follows.

In addition to the brain stem, limbic system, and cortex, teachers and caregivers can benefit from knowing about several other structures: the corpus callosum, the cerebellum, and the four structures of the limbic system.

The *corpus callosum* is a band of fibers that connects the right and left hemispheres, allowing information to be sent back and forth between the hemispheres. The *cerebellum* is the area of the brain that houses many automatic, learned functions such as maintaining one's balance, riding a bike, and unconsciously knowing how high to lift your foot to walk up a flight of stairs.

The four structures within the limbic system serve different functions:

- *Amygdala*—This almond-shaped structure is your brain's alarm system. You have two amygdalae, one in each hemisphere. These structures are constantly monitoring your environment for any threat to your survival. The amygdala is the seat of the flight, fight, or freeze decisions that every person, child or adult,

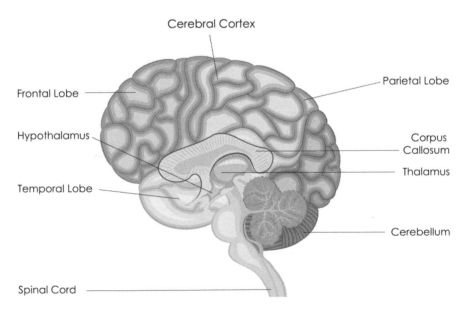

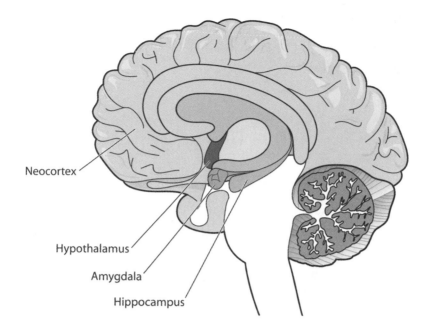

Neocortex

Hypothalamus

Amygdala

Hippocampus

must make in the face of a threat. Once activated, the amygdala takes a primary position in the way your body allocates energy. Survival trumps all.

- *Hippocampus*—This portion of the brain is critical to the storage of new memories. Again, you actually have two hippocampi. For teachers of any age level, knowing about this structure is key to promoting learning. The hippocampus works like a filing system, determining first if something is worth remembering and then determining where to file it so that this particular memory can be found again. Caregivers can help by capturing a child's interest and making the information worth remembering. You can also clarify and organize information so a child will be better able to file it. Repetition is the key to strengthening an experience so that the child forms a stronger and stronger memory. In addition, you can encourage the creation of links, so learners will be likely to find the information they have stored in their memories. Of the structures in the limbic area, the hippocampus is slow to develop and does not come fully online until ages three to five, depending on the child and the emotional strength of an early memory.

- *Thalamus*—This structure looks like and is about the size of a walnut. It serves as a primary processor of most incoming information entering the brain. It functions like a relay station, directing incoming information for further processing. The thalamus is continuously monitoring the external environment.

- *Hypothalamus*—This olive-sized structure is constantly monitoring the body's internal environment for input. The hypothalamus regulates many of the hormones of the body.

Characteristics That All Brains Share

You now know the sequence of brain development, some useful facts about the structures found in a brain, and the function of each part. In addition, knowing six characteristics of the brain will help you understand how it operates. The brain is characterized as follows:

- An adaptation organ—Brains are built to adapt in order to stay alive. The survival instinct is extremely powerful, with the brain learning and storing experiences in memory, in large part to increase your chances of surviving. The rapid speed with which a young brain adapts allows for maximum advantage to be gained for any particular setting, climate, or culture a baby happens to be born into. And the brain changes physically when it learns something. Early learning takes place so rapidly because nearly everything is new and must be explored and experienced to increase the probability of survival.

- A novelty-seeking organ—Directly related to survival is the need to seek out novel experiences. Brains attend most carefully when exposed to new objects, new sights, new sounds, and new people. The focus is on making a primal friend-or-foe assessment. "What is this new item?" "Can I eat it? Or might it eat me?" "What can I do with it?" Very young children are masters of paying attention to novel experiences. Once the child has categorized the experience, however, her attention moves quickly to the next new encounter.

- A pattern-seeking organ—When you can detect a pattern of how something works, you can better predict what will come next. A brain naturally seeks the patterns that exist in each new experience. Being able to make such predictions, including identifying whether you can count on someone, is essential to survival. Basic trust boils down to the brain determining, "Because this person behaves in a pattern and I recognize that pattern, I can figure out what is likely to happen next." Of course, many important skills needed for successfully managing your life are also organized in patterns. Pattern detection, whether it is focused on music, math, reading, or something more primal such as trust, can help us unconsciously manage our environment better.

- A pleasure-seeking organ—At the most basic level, humans prefer pleasure over pain, and we go to great lengths to satisfy that desire. Young babies who receive love and good care don't have to go far; they are pleased by a smiling face and a soothing, familiar voice; a warm blanket; and a reassuring rocking motion. As a child grows and begins to explore, the mere act of discovery and the developing sense of mastery over his environment also bring pleasure. Recent neuroscience discoveries tell us that pleasure has its own identifiable brain markers. Pleasure releases a cocktail of chemicals in the brain when humans of any age experience it. Then we want those positive feelings to come again. A child's familiar chant of "Do it again!" reminds us that the desire to reexperience pleasure is a driving force of any brain, at any age.

- An energy-conserving organ—Brains automatically shift energy to the systems that are currently being used. Brains also conserve energy and save it whenever possible to allow for future emergency needs. The body has only a given amount of energy at a given time. When more energy is being used by one function, less energy is available for other functions. This conservation-of-energy principle can help explain how energy is allocated to learning tasks as well.

- A meaning-seeking organ—To make sense of the flood of information coming from all of our senses, the brain tries to organize each and every bit into something meaningful. Experiences and sensations that are repeated form the foundations for later concepts, ideas, beliefs, and explanations of how the world works. At first, the brain notes pure, basic associations of two things occurring at the same time. (Example: "When I cry, Mom will come.") This type of learning (associative learning) continues throughout one's lifetime and represents a large amount of what each of us knows.

Another type of sense making called *cause-and-effect learning* begins between seven and twelve months. Endless hours of experimenting with what causes something to happen can help children come to conclusions that make sense to them. "What happens when I drop my toy from my high chair? Does it fall the same way every time?" "Does Nana frown at me every time I touch her crystal vase?" "Will this egg break if I drop it from the countertop?" Children conduct endless experiments to determine "What happens if. . . ."

Now that you have a foundation of information about how the brain operates, you can get more details from the resources mentioned throughout the book.

Resources

Burns, Martha. 2011. "Left vs. Right: What Your Brain Hemispheres Are Really Up To." *Scientific Learning.* http://www.scilearn.com/blog/left-brain-right-brain-hemispheres

Neville, Helen J., and Daphne Bavelier. 1998. "Neural Organization and Plasticity of Language." *Current Opinion in Neurobiology* 8(2): 254–258.

PART 2
Link What You Learn to What You Do

As a caregiver, you have the important responsibility of helping develop children's brains. That means that you need to learn how to keep children safe and provide proper stimulation. This book can help you understand how to do both, with the brain in mind.

Development Linked to Timing and Activities

Some of the ideas discussed in this book hinge on specific timing. Some do not. Certain aspects of brain development need to occur during specific time frames. This is why timing matters. Attachment is one example. Feeling safe, secure, and loved is important at every stage in a child's life. But bonding must occur early because the limbic system wires up almost entirely from birth to age five. Bonding is crucial to the continued normal development of other structures and learning processes in the brain. It's not just nice to have secure early attachments to live a healthy, happy life; it is essential.

Many other ideas depend on activities to stimulate the brain. Reading lots of colorful books, building with plastic connecting blocks, and learning to play a violin at an early age are all wonderful opportunities for a child. Engaging in these kinds of activities strengthens learning connections and promotes creativity. However, whether little Alana learns to play violin at age three, six, or ten does not determine if she will become a concert violinist. Many activities are interchangeable in that engaging a child in one or the other can easily bring about the same, or similar, brain changes. Knowing the difference between what is essential (tied to timing) and what is effective (promoted by activities) will help you evaluate and decide what to do next to benefit every child and why.

Learn, Link, Think, and Apply

You have already learned about the sequence of brain development, the key structures and functions, and the shared characteristics of all brains. Next, it will be useful for you to link this information to what you already know. Researchers call this prior knowledge, and you have lots of it! You likely have good instincts, which may be partially the result of some good parenting you received as a young child. You may have worked with young children for several years and learned by trial and error what works well and what does not. You may have taken some classes, training, or mentoring from others that guided you in knowing how to provide care. Most likely, you will bring together some combination of all those factors.

This prior knowledge resides in your existing brain networks. Now, you can build on those networks by attaching new information and creating useful, expanded understandings.

Take some time now to think. The ideas in this book are summarized in fifty-two Brain Nuggets. If you consider one idea each week, then by next year, you will have made strides toward changing your own brain networks. Or you might choose to think about several ideas in one week that in your mind fit together well. Feel free to chunk your learning and thinking into bigger ideas. The most important aspect of thinking is taking your time. Thinking and learning occur best when you take the time to reflect on what the new information means to you.

Try to apply your thinking about the brains of children to the everyday actions and activities you do with them. There is no one formula for getting it right. You know the children in your care. You know yourself. You know what others expect of you. Implement what you learn from this book as you start to feel secure in your newly constructed knowledge. Caregivers and early childhood teachers organize experiences for young children in many ways that have proven to be successful (see Table 1), but often they can't explain the larger reasons, or learning principles, behind their actions. Until recently, few of us understood the neurological reasons why approaches were successful. As you look at the actions taken by teachers and caregivers in Table 1, you should be able to recognize strategies you use with children every day. The column on the far right will help you better understand what is going on in children's brains.

Action	Learning Principles	Why
Introduce children to new objects, new words, and new concepts.	Prior knowledge is critical to future learning, and connecting new to old helps students retain information.	Neurons connect in ways that link similar ideas into networks of neurons that then fire in patterns.
Create opportunities for review sessions, repeating main ideas frequently.	Repetition improves memory.	Repetition speeds up the brain's energy flow by reducing resistance and therefore improving efficiency.
Create positive environments that emphasize positive verbal statements, building of trust, and a relaxed and calm atmosphere.	Emotion drives attention, and attention drives memory.	The brain constantly monitors the outside environment to maintain a sense of security and safety.
Incorporate fun and excitement into your lessons and into daily activities.	Emotion drives attention, and attention drives memory.	The brain seeks pleasure and seeks to repeat pleasurable experiences.
Plan your day to provide multiple experiences with information (listening, reading, acting out, talking, and moving).	Active participation improves retention of info; multiple modes of encoding improve retention.	Information encoded redundantly has multiple retrieval routes, providing more ways to find information later.
Organize new information by giving previews and pictures of what is coming next, logically sequencing information.	Organizing information helps to store it efficiently.	The brain has processing limitations that can be overcome by grouping information during storage.
Remember that your child care curriculum is sequenced to introduce different kinds of experiences and different types of learning at different ages.	Readiness is an important consideration for skill acquisition.	The brain develops dynamically and follows a progression (back to front, inside to outside, and bottom to top) that influences capabilities.
Utilize routines and create rituals when organizing expectations for the classroom.	Routines free up the system to focus on new information.	The brain is constantly seeking to find a pattern in experiences.
Use pictures, diagrams, charts, maps, and symbols to teach many concepts.	Visual images aid memory.	Images help overcome processing limitations. It is easier to recall images than written words, as many parts of an image can be grouped together as one.
Present information in multiple ways, and help learners to create connections to prior experiences.	Learners construct their own meaning and, therefore, knowledge.	Brains develop uniquely in response to incoming stimuli, based on prior connections. Brains search for cause-and-effect explanations. Humans create meaning when necessary.

PART 3
General Science-Based Messages

⚡ 1. Use it or lose it.

How will knowing this help me?

Brain connections grow based on experiences. When you learn something and a neural connection is first formed, that connection can be vulnerable and unstable. However, you strengthen those new connections each time you repeat what you have learned. More and more practice continues to strengthen the connections and begins to secure the learning for long periods of time. Connections reinforced through repeated use tend to stay active and available.

Connections that begin in one brain area become connected to other regions and form circuits. When the information contained within the circuits is used, the circuits and networks that have been wired together and are connected will fire together, thereby activating all parts of the network. When information is not used for a long time, the connections become weaker. Eventually, the circuits may no longer fire when the network is activated, and the connection will be lost. This loss of connectedness is a part of what is called *neural pruning*. This

BRAIN NUGGET

When it comes to brain function, use it or lose it is the rule. Neural circuits and networks in the brain grow stronger with use and weaker when inactive.

pruning is a natural process of eliminating connections that are no longer used or useful in the brain. Because these connections can fade away, repetition and reinforcement are important to maintaining learning.

So what should I try to do?

Provide lots of opportunities for children to practice what they learn. Short exposure to new experiences may not be sufficient to secure long-term benefits. You can strengthen connections in several ways:

- Do it again. Repeat the experience. Practice. Try again. Reinforce through repetition.

- Bring the experience back into the child's memory. Prompt the child to talk about, read about, act out, or draw what happened. Try different combinations of re-experiencing to find what works with a particular child.

- Extend the initial learning. Create similar experiences. Remember to explicitly link the new learning to prior, similar experiences. This tends to build an elaborated network of similar concepts in the child's brain. The new experience will remind the child of something he already knows. This not only feels good but also builds conceptual knowledge that the child can later use in multiple ways.

- Contrast the first experience with other experiences the child has had that are very different. Highlight exactly how the new experience differs from a prior experience.

⚡ 2. Pay attention to the sequence and timing of how a new brain wires up.

How will knowing this help me?

As you learned in the Brain Basics 101 section, a new brain develops in a sequence that is driven by our biology. Brains develop from the back to the front, from the inside out, and from the bottom up. Knowing this sequence can help you know where best to place your efforts in helping children get the stimulation they need at optimal times.

From the Back to the Front

- Vision develops early. Be sure that normal visual input is available to babies in the first six months while their visual system is wiring so rapidly.

- Auditory discrimination, which means being able to hear individual sounds clearly, wires rapidly during the first several years. It is important to get the child a hearing screening if a parent or caregiver suspects a problem. Children need to be able to hear the small differences in speech sounds that are the building blocks of language.

> **BRAIN NUGGET**
>
> The earlier a system wires up, the more resistant it is to change. It is not impossible to change some brain structures later in life, but the early developing systems are difficult to change.

- Motor development refines movements throughout childhood, but babies and toddlers need freedom to move and explore. Avoid restraining them too much. Yes, safety is important, but there must be a balance that allows freedom of body movements to naturally build the strength and flexibility needed for typical motor advancements.

- Thinking, reasoning, and decision-making skills progress throughout childhood, accelerate during adolescence, and peak in young adulthood.

From the Inside Out

- The brain stem and limbic system wire up before most of the neocortex. The important regulatory functions such as breathing, heart rate, and temperature regulation develop before the sensory areas that process vision, hearing, movement, and so on.

- The emotional processing centers that are located deep in the center of the brain wire rapidly and are well established from birth to five years old. Environments that are safe and relationships that are loving, stimulating, predictable, and responsive to a child's needs build better, healthier brains.

From the Bottom Up

- The brain stem—critical for the regulation of breathing, heart rate, temperature, and other life-sustaining functions—is already well developed in a full-term, healthy baby.

- Sensory brain regions continue to develop throughout childhood, adolescence, and beyond. These sensory, or somesthetic, areas are housed in the neocortex of the brain.

- Brain circuits continue to develop toward the upper areas of cortical brain regions, including the continuous development of the sensory-motor strip that sits at the top and outer side areas of the brain. This area stretches across the top of your head where a wide headband might stretch if it went from ear to ear.

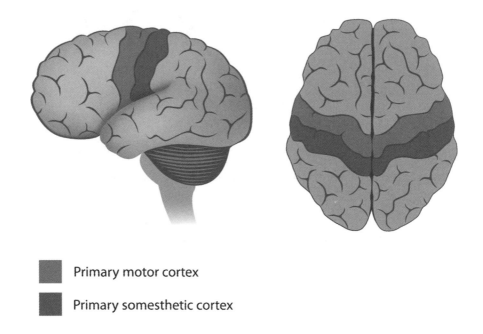

■ Primary motor cortex

■ Primary somesthetic cortex

So what should I try to do?

Knowing the sequence of development will help you to have more realistic expectations for what skills you think a child should be taught and when. Not realizing that the brain circuits needed to support these capacities may not be ready, you might create problems by holding unrealistic expectations. Children can't always share nicely as two-year-olds or resist grabbing toys they want. Young children may struggle to sit quietly

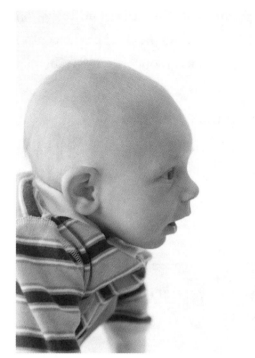

and listen to us present information in a group for twenty minutes or more. We may be rushing development by trying to teach a three-year-old to read or to learn abstract math concepts. We sometimes continue to have unrealistic expectations throughout childhood and into adolescence, when we expect teens to be consistent in making wise choices or to avoid experimenting with risky behaviors.

Most important, if you know the sequence of development, you can make better choices about where to place your emphasis when you plan for various experiences with children. For example:

- You know to focus lots of attention on providing secure, predictable environments for infants and young toddlers because their limbic systems (emotional centers of the brain) are actively wiring important circuits. Many excellent care providers and parents have instinctively done this, but now you know why. When you know why something is important, you are more likely to take appropriate action on purpose instead of by accident.

- It is important to limit screen time for babies and young toddlers. The attention system wires up early, and quick hits of information (such as commercials on television) do not promote the development of a longer attention span.

- Infants and toddlers do not learn language from watching television. Television speech happens way too fast for adequate processing, and the child has no control over being able to stop or slow down the input, and no opportunity to interact with or control the images on the screen.

- Children need to have the opportunity to hear distinct language sounds as infants and toddlers to develop what is known as *phonemic awareness*. Therefore, it is important to tend to ear infections quickly so that a child's brain is receiving clear auditory input.

⚡ 3. Don't expect to see brain structures change, but know that they do so continuously.

How will knowing this help me?

Neuroscientists have known for some time that physical changes occur in the brain when a person learns something, but this idea takes some getting used to for most of us.

As a result of new experiences and sensory input—or repetition of the input— parts of the neuron grow and connect in unique ways. The neuron grows new branches in what are called *dendrites* as more stimulation is received. This growth resembles a tree that is adding new branches and filling out. Likewise, at the

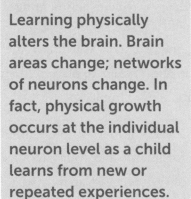

BRAIN NUGGET

Learning physically alters the brain. Brain areas change; networks of neurons change. In fact, physical growth occurs at the individual neuron level as a child learns from new or repeated experiences.

tip of the *axon*, or nerve fiber, that sends stimulation out to other neurons, tiny structures actually change from a round, Tootsie Pop shape to the appearance of an opened umbrella. Once the structures open, they maintain that shape. Now you can understand the ways that learning physically changes the size and shape of brain structures.

Also during learning, neurons transfer the new information as electrical charges along the axon structure. Repeated learning sparks repeated electrical activity, which triggers the development of a fatty substance called *myelin*. As myelin deposits along the axon structure, it acts as an insulator and allows electrical charges to flow faster and more efficiently. This process makes learning easier because it takes less energy to transfer the information from one part of the brain to another. You can't see this physical change happen from the outside, and yet you can see the results. You will notice the change after watching a child who struggled with something early in the learning process later accomplish that same task with little effort. The child's brain underwent change as a result of stimulation, repetition, and practice.

So what should I try to do?

- Realize the power you have to shape the brain development of every child in your care. Words, concepts, experiences, interaction patterns, and emotions that you provide through the relationships you create will make a difference in the future trajectory of a child's mind.

- Be mindful. Be aware that what you do matters every day.

- Knowing that the brain actually grows new wiring in response to what happens to a child can give you a tremendous new sense of purpose. It is a powerful responsibility! As you make decisions about how best to interact with individuals or groups of children, you can creatively enhance their world.

⚡ 4. Realize that varying levels of stress cause different reactions in the brain.

How will knowing this help me?

Stress is a part of each of our lives, but the degree of stress that a person experiences can cause very different responses in the brain. Also, the age at which a person experiences high doses of stress can result in a dramatically different brain architecture and brain circuitry. Early exposure to significant stressors can have a negative impact on brain structure and function that is difficult to reverse.

Child-development experts categorize the degrees of stress that children can experience into three levels:

- *Positive stress* is common and is triggered by mildly stressful events, such as breaking a favorite toy or missing a party because of illness. When faced with everyday stressors, a child's brain will experience a short-term, moderate stress response. The difficulty will be experienced and will pass quickly, and the child's emotional state will return to her baseline, or where she normally functions.

BRAIN NUGGET

Although mild stress is experienced by all people, excessive stressors that occur early in life can have damaging outcomes that are difficult to repair. With too much stress or fear, the receptors for learning shut down.

- *Tolerable stress* can be strong and significant. For example, stressors might include a child losing a parent, experiencing the parents' divorce, or moving to a new home far away from current friends and family. These experiences, however, can be mitigated and eased by caring adults who can significantly buffer the continued impact of the stressor. Supportive relationships play a major role in helping a child recover from this level of stress.

- *Toxic stress* results from long-term, strong, and recurring adverse circumstances. Recurring threats to a person's survival such as those experienced in war zones, in a chaotic and erratic home life, with physical or sexual abuse, and with long-term neglect can have devastating effects on the developing brain of a child. Brains can be smaller in size, and brain structures, such as the amygdala and hippocampus (see Brain Basics 101), can be smaller or less reliable in their functioning. Children exposed to toxic stress will need long-term help from qualified professionals to begin to resolve and repair significant issues for better future functioning. Supportive relationships from caring adults become mandatory along with professional guidance.

So what should I try to do?

The duration and intensity of stressful experiences can make the difference between healthy development and lasting trauma-related damage. As a caregiver, you can provide many valuable supports to a child who may be experiencing one or more of these levels.

- Children will experience positive stress nearly every day. The routines and rituals you already have in place will provide external regulation that is critical in helping a child calm down and regain a sense of internal regulation. Rules and schedules provide the comfort that a child often needs to change her focus to other things and let go of the current worry. Your ability to show love and empathy tells the child that you recognize and understand her pain. Then she may be able to move on and have a great day!

- Reading stories about other children or storybook characters who are experiencing similar challenges can begin to reduce positive stress and help a child feel less alone with a problem. Knowing that others have had the same troubles can help.

- When identifying tolerable stress, consult a child's family so you can coordinate consistent messaging and reinforce one another's efforts to help the child to recover. You may experience more, or possibly less, acting out or withdrawing than the child exhibits at home. Involving others (perhaps a supervisor or director in group child care settings) will ensure consistent treatment that can be provided with or without outside professional guidance.

- When a child in your care is exhibiting signs of toxic stress, such as withdrawal or emotional outbursts, it is critical that you consult with directors, family advocates, and advisors to share the burden of comprehensive planning and intervention.

Resources

Center on the Developing Child. 2015. "Toxic Stress." Center on the Developing Child, Harvard University, accessed September 23, 2015. http://developingchild .harvard.edu/science/key-concepts/toxic-stress/

Perry, Bruce D., et al. 1995. "Childhood Trauma, the Neurobiology of Adaptation, and 'Use-Dependent' Development of the Brain: How 'States' Become 'Traits.'" *Infant Mental Health Journal* 16(4): 271–292.

⚡ 5. Link new ideas you want children to learn to things they already know.

How will knowing this help me?

Learning something new takes lots of energy in the brain. New connections are forged and then later are made stronger through practice. The best way to secure new learning is to connect it to something a child already knows.

What is happening in the brain when you purposefully link the new with the existing knowledge is that the new piece of information is not isolated, but rather is linked in and physically wired into a network of related information. Information that is integrated into an existing network then gets activated each time the network fires. This process is best explained by the common neuroscience statement, "Neurons that fire together wire together." The same neurons that have been linked now all fire at the same time, and the new information gains strength from being in the network.

So what should I try to do?

- When you introduce a new word or a new idea, ask a child what he might already know about it. See if it reminds him of something already seen or heard.

- Use visuals, such as photos or objects, to help you explain new concepts. Sometimes a visual cue will activate a memory for a child that will help link new and existing ideas.

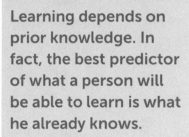

BRAIN NUGGET

Learning depends on prior knowledge. In fact, the best predictor of what a person will be able to learn is what he already knows.

- Introduce the same idea using multiple modalities; some children learn better through one sense or another. Talk about it, draw it, act it out, sing about it, or dance it out. You get the idea. Think of ways of using sight, sound, and movement to secure new learning. Later, when a child tries to remember something, there will be multiple roads leading to the knowledge that is stored and distributed in multiple areas of the brain.

- As a caregiver, you already have brain networks that hold your prior knowledge about caring for young children, and you can use those existing frameworks to hang new information on and expand your understanding. Do the same with children. Use the existing networks children have as a framework, and add new information to increase their understanding and their memory abilities.

⚡ 6. Be aware of how many skills depend on pattern recognition.

How will knowing this help me?

Many things in life occur in patterns. Some are naturally occurring phenomena, and others are created by humans to make life more manageable and less chaotic. Once a pattern is discovered, learning about a topic or procedure can be much easier. We can better sort and understand incoming data because we automatically analyze things by recognizing patterns. Successful learners use them to organize their world better.

We are built to find meaning in the patterns we identify. This tendency is so powerful that we sometimes ascribe meaning to a particular pattern that does not fit. That is how some superstitions arise; we decide that events are following a pattern that does not actually exist!

So what should I try to do?

For fun, practice your skills in identifying patterns by noting those that nature provides:

- Patterns in the florets of many flowers and plants
- Honeycomb formations in a beehive
- Zebra stripes
- Snowflakes
- Crystal rock symmetries

One of the earliest patterns that babies' brains learn is that when they cry, someone will come to help meet their needs. Note: This differs from spoiling. The baby is making a basic association that recognizes a pattern of response, not manipulating. The brain of an infant is not yet capable of manipulation.

Think about some patterns encountered in other areas of life and learning:

- Music
- Multiplication tables
- The ten-digit counting system
- Reading
- Grammar and speech
- Behavior

You can help children begin to look for patterns if you point them out in various fun activities.

BRAIN NUGGET

The brain is a pattern-seeking organ. Knowing this can make learning easier.

- Many toddlers love to pull things out and line them up. When the child is at home, start a pattern of shoes such as Daddy's shoe, big sister's shoe, the child's own shoe, Daddy's, sister's, child's, Daddy's, sister's, child's, and so on. She will be entertained for long periods of time pulling the shoes out of the closet, dragging them to the family room or kitchen, and lining them up in a pattern. If you get really lucky, she may help put them all back!

- Before eating snacks, form a pattern on a plate with colored cereal or other foods with simple color variations, and then let the child extend the pattern before eating the snack. Start with a simple pattern of red-yellow, red-yellow, red-yellow. Once the child shows success in continuing that pattern, you can increase the difficulty just a bit to red-yellow-blue, red-yellow-blue, and so on. Challenge older children to replicate more complex patterns, such as red-red-blue-green, red-red-blue-green, and so on.

- With older children, point out how our number system uses digits *1* through *9* before the base *10* and then repeats those digits in the same pattern in the twenties, thirties, and forties, and so on.

- You can help children recognize more abstract patterns, such as how stories in books follow the sequence of beginning, middle, and end. Learning to keep conceptual information in a useful order is a skill that children can benefit from in so many academic areas.

- The most helpful pattern for young children is the introduction and regular use of routines, whether at home or in group care. Routines allow people to organize daily life in predictable ways instead of experiencing the day as random or chaotic events. Routines comfort humans of all ages because they help us know what will come next. This kind of organization allows for structured expectations instead of bombarding the mind with unorganized and random input.

⚡ 7. Know why tummy time is recommended by pediatricians.

How will knowing this help me?

For more than fifteen years, health officials and pediatricians have advised that babies should be put to sleep on their backs as a precaution against Sudden Infant Death Syndrome, known as SIDS. Of course, caregivers should follow this important recommendation. It is also important for babies to experience the feeling of being on their stomachs. Therefore, caregivers should place babies on their tummies on purpose during the day so the babies can move in ways that can help their overall development.

For example, when a baby begins to lift his head, the neck and upper-back muscles strengthen. These muscles are needed for the baby to roll over, sit up, and crawl. Strong muscles also allow babies to turn their heads to see what is happening around them and to have a different view of the world. To increase muscle strength and opportunities for varied cognitive perspectives, tummy time can help with physical and mental development.

So what should I try to do?

> **BRAIN NUGGET**
>
> While a baby is awake and alert, encourage deliberate activities that require tummy time because most babies are not spending sufficient time on their stomachs.

- Always supervise a baby or young toddler during tummy time to be sure he is safe. Be present. Stay alert.

- Because many babies are not familiar with the feeling of being on the tummy, they will fuss at first. Start by laying the infant across your lap. Once the baby tolerates this, gradually move to a blanket or mat on the floor. Play, while on the stomach, can be planned for five or ten minutes several times a day. The more practice, the better the baby will like it.

- Tummy time is especially important to schedule during the first year of life. Planning mindfully to do fun activities while the baby is on his tummy will help to ensure that valuable practice occurs. Playing with age-appropriate colorful toys or seeing your face up close during interactions will often keep a child engaged.

- During waking hours, time spent on the tummy will also help keep the baby from developing a flat spot on an otherwise rounded head. Babies who spend most of their awake time and asleep time on their backs are vulnerable to developing a flat spot. Be assured, however, that such a deviation in head shape has no cognitive deficit associated with it.

⚡ 8. Encourage activities that cross the midline of the body.

How will knowing this help me?

Crawling is an excellent start to a series of many future movements that occur in reciprocal patterns requiring the alternate use of one side of the brain and then the other. Walking, running, climbing, skipping, riding a bicycle, and dancing all require the coordination of alternating use of the right and the left sides of the body. The left hemisphere of the brain controls the right leg, arm, and hand, and the right hemisphere controls the left ones.

When the alternating use of body parts crosses the imaginary center line of the body—called the *midline*—the brain gets practice connecting input and output from one hemisphere to the other. With practice, brain connections become stronger. Movements smooth out, become faster, and take less energy. When it comes to crawling, eventually this automatic pattern takes very little mental energy, so the child can use that energy for other things, such as learning!

Although crawling has many benefits, some children skip this stage almost entirely and move straight to walking. Do not panic. Children will have many opportunities to experience crossing the midline and to practice reciprocal patterns of body movements. Continue to think of other ways their movements will cross the midline while they play. At the same time, be sensitive to exuberant parents who think that if children walk early, they are supersmart and ahead of the class. Encouraging children to move is good, but early walking usually is not a sign of anything other than early walking.

So what should I try to do?

- When working with babies, encourage tummy time. This is a perfect way to strengthen the muscles that support the body for crawling.

- When working with young toddlers, provide lots of opportunities to keep them moving on the floor in ways that encourage not only crawling, but also rolling and moving around during play.

- For preschoolers, add more cross-lateral-movement sequences in the games you play. For example, when playing Simon Says, create a movement of crossing your arms over your chest or crossing your hands and touching your knees. Also, toddlers and preschoolers love to dance to music. Many commercially available CDs have songs that specifically target gross motor movement in various sequences. Such song and dance experiences also stimulate the use of both hemispheres of the brain.

BRAIN NUGGET

Crawling is an excellent activity for young children because the coordination of the movements to crawl activates both hemispheres of the brain and strengthens the connective structure in the brain known as the corpus callosum.

⚡ 9. Remain hopeful that every child can benefit permanently by living in positive environments.

How will knowing this help me?

This idea is not as complicated as it sounds. Each of us is born with a set of genes that we inherited from our parents, grandparents, and ancestors. Most of us are familiar with this notion of inheritance as well as the fact that each person's configuration of genes (DNA) is unique. Television programs commonly entertain us with the discovery of someone's DNA found from collecting saliva, hair, or skin cells.

A new understanding of DNA, known as *epigenetics*, has found that even though a person is born with particular genes, those genes may or may not express themselves. In other words, they may be activated or remain dormant. The big discovery in science is that experiences can influence whether or not some genes get turned on. This information is helping scientists to understand why certain environments tend to create undesirable characteristics,

BRAIN NUGGET

A person's genetic material is not static. Experiences can influence gene expression.

such as extremely aggressive tendencies. Other environments, such as loving, predictable ones, are conducive to gene expression that leads to better self-regulation abilities. Stay tuned. Scientific advances may soon be able to do more than suggest optimal environments for healthy brain development; they may be able to define desirable environments with more and more precision.

So what should I try to do?

- Create positive environments that enhance the probability of children bonding with others, empathizing with others, learning how to pay attention, and beginning the process of self-regulation. Poorly organized environments that easily become chaotic have little consistency, have few routines and procedures that children can count on, and are stressful to teachers and children. Avoid these environments because they may trigger unwanted characteristics in the brains of developing children.

- Remain hopeful that every child, with a combination of love and supportive environments, can develop in healthy ways. You can strive to break the cycle of generational dysfunction by providing positive experiences and promoting healthy patterns among children, especially those with multiple risk factors.

- Supportive relationships can buffer negative effects caused by stress, and you can be that buffer.

Resources

Suomi, Stephen J. 2003. "Gene-Environment Interactions and the Neurobiology of Social Conflict." *Annals of the New York Academy of Sciences* 1008: 132–139.

Valeo, Tom. 2009. "Frontier: Environment Influences Gene Expression." *BrainWork.* http://www.dana.org/Publications/Brainwork/Details.aspx?id=43767

⚡ 10. Resist the natural temptation to look for a quick fix.

How will knowing this help me?

You have probably heard the old adage "If it sounds too good to be true, it probably is!" This holds true for ideas and products that promise parents and caregivers a magic pill that can teach a child to read at one year or that can make a toddler sleep contentedly after one week in a crib located down the hall from her mother. These promises are tempting to be sure. The reality is that there are few shortcuts to providing attention and responsive relationships when it comes to young children. Children need both time and attention from caring adults to internalize lifelong capacities for empathy, self-regulation, social-emotional competence, and positive self-regard.

What is so seductive about many quick fixes is that they promise to free up time needed for adult tasks. Alternatively, the quick fix may promise achievements for children that will translate to academic or monetary success for years to come.

In a quest to do the right thing, many parents of infants and young toddlers start searching for that magic pill, embracing the next expensive program that will promise a high IQ. They approach the quest as if the answer is somewhere out there in retail land, when really it comes from the relationship they can form with their own child. They will work magic when they establish consistent, predictable response patterns early in their interactions with the child.

So what should I try to do?

- Avoid the temptation to jump on board when an idea or program goes against your prior experiences with young children, especially if it sounds too easy. Caring for children is rewarding, challenging, complex, time-consuming, exciting, and life affirming, but it is seldom easy. Part of the joy comes from realizing that your efforts have been integral in helping them grow into thinking, caring, and loving adults.

BRAIN NUGGET

Before you purchase child-development products that promise to make children supersmart, carefully examine them. Buyer beware.

- Before investing emotionally or financially in a new product, approach, or program, look to see if there is reliable research to support it. Many universities and child-development and child-advocacy groups can serve as good sources of information about promising ideas and programs that work. The most important component of any formula for success always starts with providing a sense of safety, security, and attention that allows children to know they are loved, cared for, seen, and heard. And you can't bottle that!

⚡ 11. Be able to explain the early childhood return on investment.

How will knowing this help me?

Often, those who provide direct care for children from birth to five years old have little awareness of the potential economic benefits their service provides. Economist James Heckman, a Nobel Prize winner, provides a detailed analysis of how monies invested in high-quality care in the early years can offer future savings by avoiding expensive rehabilitative services. From a purely economic perspective, it is smart to invest in early education for the entire population. From a human perspective, it is the right thing to do because competent, self-confident people lead more productive and satisfying lives.

In earlier research, Arthur Rolnick and Rob Grunewald of the Federal Reserve Bank of Minneapolis found that, "Careful academic research demonstrates that tax dollars spent on early childhood development provide extraordinary returns compared with investments in the public, and even private, sector," as reported in a study titled "Early Intervention on a Large Scale." The benefits include the potential for the participating children to earn higher wages as adults. Rolnick notes that "the broader economy also benefits because individuals who participate in high-quality early childhood development programs have greater skills than they otherwise would, and they're able to contribute productively to their local economies."

So what should I try to do?

- After realizing the power of this economic argument, spread this information to friends and family members who may not realize the far-reaching value of providing early care and education to young children.

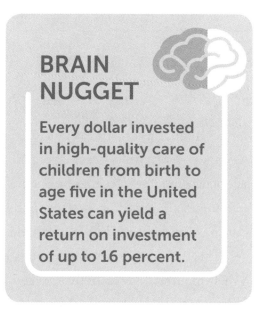

BRAIN NUGGET

Every dollar invested in high-quality care of children from birth to age five in the United States can yield a return on investment of up to 16 percent.

- Continue to provide learning environments that foster motivation and persistence because these are skills that business leaders recognize as directly applicable to their workforce needs.

- Continue to give children learning opportunities that provide practice in the development of executive functions because these abilities to organize, prioritize, and solve problems have their origins in early childhood. A healthy society depends on having citizens who are competent in these skills.

Resources

Heckman, James J., and Dimitriy V. Masterov. 2007. "The Productivity Argument for Investing in Young Children." *Review of Agricultural Economics* 29(3): 446–493.

InvestMN. 2012. "Begin at the Beginning." *Talking Points*. http://www.massp.org /downloads_massp/investmn/talking_points/InvestMN_Feb_2012_Beginning

Rolnick, Arthur J., and Rob Grunewald. 2007. "Early Intervention on a Large Scale." Federal Reserve Bank of Minneapolis *Special Studies*. https://www. minneapolisfed.org/publications/special-studies/early-childhood-development/ early-intervention-on-a-large-scale

Rolnick, Arthur J., and Rob Grunewald. 2003. "Early Childhood Development = Economic Development." Federal Reserve Bank of Minneapolis *fedgazette*. https://www.minneapolisfed.org/publications/fedgazette/early-childhood -development-economic-development

---

⚡ 12. See the brain as a novelty-seeking organ.

How will knowing this help me?

In the Brain Basics 101 section of this book, you may have already learned that the brain is a novelty-seeking organ. New objects, new things, new people, new experiences, and new feelings hold a preferential place in the way humans explore their environment. Everything is tested for its usefulness. The primary survival question that is unconsciously being asked at each moment of discovery is, "Can I eat it, or will it eat me?" This important questioning starts early. Babies test everything by putting things in their mouths. They learn the size and shape of an object, for example, by tasting it to see how it feels in their mouths and by feeling it with their hands. The brain begins to map objects by integrating the sight, sound, feel, and taste of them.

Whether you are planning a game, designing an art project, or reading a book with a child, variety can be the spice of life. Children love novel experiences. New objects and new people capture their attention in compelling ways. The new child in the group, the new toy, the new dog, and the new book all hold power over a young child's interest.

Yet humans are soothed by the familiar. When something is familiar to you, your brain doesn't have to work so hard. You have already expended the energy to learn about it, and you don't have to worry whether it is going to hurt you in any way. You can relax in the knowledge that the familiar is the known. A child's comfy old blanket, favorite doll, or favorite story all hold a special preference in the mind.

BRAIN NUGGET

Choose both variety and familiarity when playing with or reading to a child. The brain is turned on by both the familiar and the new.

So what should I try to do?

- For babies, sing or play favorite songs as cues that can signal certain desired behaviors. Familiar songs can set the mood for sleeping, waking up, or celebrating. Those melodies can be reassuring.

- Introduce new things and new people by allowing the child time to get to know them. Newness can be exhilarating or overwhelming, depending on a child's temperament.

- Circulate toys and books in and out of sight so that a child can feel glad to see an old friend in the form of a toy or book but can be stimulated by new items you add into the cycle.

- Know that children need to explore objects introduced to them. They must! The brain will not be satisfied until the child gains a level of understanding about the new item.

⚡ 13. Understand how play is linked directly to learning.

How will knowing this help me?

Over the years, many critics of early childhood education have complained that the only thing children do all day in preschool is play. Few of us have known exactly how to respond convincingly with any data other than our own experiences that tell us we are right; play is the primary way children learn. Now neuroscience can help us explain to parents and community leaders this direct relationship: The repetition in play leads to learning. Children do not want to repeat tedious or unpleasant things; they want to repeat things that are fun and interesting or that challenge them to keep trying.

In the brain, when we repeat a connection, it grows stronger. The energy needed to make that connection travels more easily and faster each time we repeat the connection. As the connection happens again and again, more and more myelin (a fatty substance that acts like insulation on a wire) is laid down along the neuron, helping energy to flow more easily, and the child gets better at that task. It is beautiful how it all works.

So what should I try to do?

- Encourage play. Keep activities open ended as much as possible. Provide experiences that young children will want to repeat.

- Be sure that children can become successful. By preschool, they enjoy tasks more when they are at least 80 percent successful. If the success rate is lower, the child is not as likely to persist. So provide some challenge, but let the child feel successful with his achievement.

> **BRAIN NUGGET**
>
> Why is play so important to children's learning? Play activates the pleasure centers of the brain. When something is fun and feels good, the brain wants to repeat it! And repetition actually strengthens the learning.

- Provide assistance that is just enough. This is sometimes referred to as the *zone of proximal development.* Support children's learning with minimal, helpful assistance.

- Remember this message from neuroscience about the relationship between play, repetition, and learning. It will help you confidently explain your rationale to parents and critics alike, and the children will benefit because you are a convincing advocate for play itself.

PART 4
Attention Messages

⚡ 14. Use emotion to help children pay better attention.

How will knowing this help me?

To consciously learn anything, you must first pay attention. Some things will automatically demand your attention. As caregivers, however, you are often concerned with encouraging children to give more attention and control it better.

Humans big or small direct their attention to things that feel important. So if you want to gain the attention of a child, the best thing you can do is engage the child's emotions. You don't have to create situations in which the emotions are too intense—superhappy, superscary, or supersad—to accomplish this. Instead, create learning environments that are exciting and where children have developed an expectation that wonderful, interesting things are going to happen.

When children's lives are filled with happiness, excitement, and joy, the channels for learning open wide. Research has shown that the brain encodes memories that are linked to strong emotions to a greater degree than memories of the ordinary, so design environments that are positive.

BRAIN NUGGET

In the brain, emotion drives attention, and attention drives memory.

So what should I try to do?

You can make things emotionally important when you purposefully link new experiences to something the child is already interested in.

- Use your voice intonation, facial expressions, and hand gestures to emphasize important words or ideas.

- Marvel at things yourself. An adult who is filled with wonder passes that right along to the children.

- Let the children see your interest in a topic and, most importantly, your interest in them. Let them know that you think something is worthwhile, and that feeling will be contagious.

- Set up learning opportunities that stimulate curiosity. When demonstrating something you want children to learn, pique their interest by asking, "What do you think is going to happen?"

- Plan everyday routines so that children can rotate being helpers. Personal attention and recognition for even small tasks of leadership can arouse great pride and fill a child with joy.

- Plan special events that bring excitement to the day. It might be something big such as a fun outing, or it could be something small such as a treasure hunt in the side yard.

Resource

McGaugh, James L. 2013. "Making Lasting Memories: Remembering the Significant." *Proceedings of the National Academy of Sciences, USA* 110(2): 10401–10407.

⚡ 15. Play fun tracking exercises with infants.

How will knowing this help me?

When a young child practices fun activities that require him to move either the eyes or body parts across the midline, which is the imaginary center line of the body, the brain gets practice in connecting input from one hemisphere to the other. The better connected the hemispheres, the easier learning becomes. Easier is better!

The left hemisphere actually controls the right side of body, and the right hemisphere controls the left side. Movements that require both hemispheres to work together bring blood and nutrients to the corpus callosum, which is the large connective band of fibers joining the hemispheres, allowing that area of the brain to develop stronger connections. Stronger is better!

BRAIN NUGGET

Activities that involve visually tracking an object and experiences that cross the midline of the body help wire the brain effectively, connecting the two hemispheres of the brain.

When a person repeats any activity that requires using both hemispheres at the same time or one after the other, different areas of the brain become more connected. Connected is better!

So what should I try to do?

If you are caring for an infant, the idea of tracking is important for several reasons:

- Check to make sure the infant can see objects within the recommended distance of 8 to 12 inches away. If you are in doubt, have parents consult a professional.

- Try to extend your playful early tracking. For example, you might move objects in a large circle. When an infant focuses on an object long enough to follow it as it moves, this helps develop the infant's attention system.

- Experiment with moving the object from the baby's left to right, as this may help to establish a preference for left-to-right eye tracking needed later for learning to read.

- As the object reaches the midline, you may notice the infant's eyes suddenly move back and forth for a moment as he tries to maintain focus on the object. This is normal, as control of the infant's gaze needs to switch from one hemisphere to the other. Repetition of the fun tracking activity will smooth this hesitation away as the brain gets practiced in this task.

⚡ 16. Get young children out of convenient safety buckets when the buckets are not necessary.

How will knowing this help me?

Of course, all young children must be kept safely strapped in a car seat in the car, but they do not need to be contained longer just for convenience. New travel systems are just that—systems. The modern car seat transfers from home to car to stroller and back again. Many other convenience contraptions such as swings, high chairs, and bouncers have their place, but you should not overuse them. Walkers, however, should not be used at all, according to the American Academy of Pediatrics' website healthychildren.org. Some child-development experts refer to these containment devices as "buckets" and advise limiting the time children spend in them. Although seemingly benign, this type of containment can restrict cognitive development as well as movement opportunities.

A critically important element of cognitive development is the attention system, which has been studied and explained by researchers Michael Posner, M. Rosario Rueda, and colleagues. In a typically developing brain, this system wires up rapidly, involving three distinct structures in three different brain regions. The first two come online in the first fourteen months—so early! The first, *alerting*, refers to the ability to devote attention to something in the environment. The second, *orienting*, refers to the ability to shift attention from one thing to another. The third component, *maintaining*, is also called executive control and involves processing conflicting or new input. This function develops by about age seven.

Babies cannot exercise their attention systems if their movements and vision are restricted by car seats and infant carriers. They cannot turn around to see what is making noise behind them. They cannot exercise the shifting function of the attention system in order to switch from one stimulus to another. The real problem is that a child soon learns that these efforts are futile and stops trying. Contrast this with a child who is held on a caregiver's hip and has a greater range of motion. This child will nearly turn upside down and backwards in an effort to investigate the interesting noise behind her.

So what should I try to do?

- If you are transporting children, they need to be strapped into safety seats. When they are not in transport, get them out and in your arms or on the floor where they are free to experience a full range of motion and where their attention system is allowed to wire naturally.

- If you work in a child care setting that is filled with buckets, begin to phase them out. Until you have done so, restrain children only when safety is a primary concern. Replace high chairs, which are convenient for adults, with low child-size chairs and tables. If a child must be in a contained holder, one that rocks or moves is preferable to a car seat.

BRAIN NUGGET

Taking a child out of the car seat when you are not traveling in a vehicle will promote her sensory learning. Freedom of movement promotes sensory integration and can encourage the normal development of the initial components of the brain's attention system.

- Other strategies include holding children in your arms when possible. They also need practice lying on their tummies while they are awake and supervised. Be mindful of the locations of other mobile children who could disrupt or injure the baby who is on the floor. Encourage babies to explore their environments because this will increase opportunities for sensory integration, which involves processing input from more than one of our senses at the same time.

Resources

Healthychildren.org. 2015. "Baby Walkers: A Dangerous Choice." *Healthychildren.org*, accessed October 4, 2015. https://www.healthychildren.org/English /safety-prevention/at-home/Pages/Baby-Walkers-A-Dangerous-Choice.aspx

Posner, Michael I., and Steven E. Petersen. 1990. "The Attention System of the Human Brain." *Annual Review of Neuroscience* 13: 25–42.

Rueda, M. Rosario, et al. 2005. "Training, Maturation, and Genetic Influences on the Development of Executive Attention." *Proceedings of the National Academy of Sciences, USA* 102(41): 14931–14936.

⚡ 17. Give children opportunities to make predictions.

How will knowing this help me?

When a human makes a prediction and that prediction turns out to be correct, his brain releases a little burst of dopamine, which is the feel-good neurotransmitter. We all function better when we can detect a pattern in our environment or in our interactions with others because we feel good when we can predict what will happen next.

Dopamine not only signals pleasure but also affects alertness (called *arousal*) and the ability to concentrate. Setting up the mental habits of being alert and able to concentrate can start at a very early age. The experience of being alert, focused, and feeling good is one we hope every child starts to prefer through lots of repetition of these sensations.

So what should I try to do?

- If you are caring for babies and toddlers, take the time to read some lift-the-flap books one-on-one with a child. After about the second or third time you show the pictures and talk about what is hiding on each page, the child will begin to remember. That is when the fun begins! Because he actually knows what is hiding under each flap, he will delight in the fact that he got it right when you reveal it again. A brain at any age just loves to be right. Right?

- If you work with older toddlers and preschoolers, use reading time to exercise the children's love of guessing what might happen to a particular character in the book. You

BRAIN NUGGET

Being able to predict what is coming next is a critical need of every brain, regardless of age. Because brains are pattern-seeking organs, people gain satisfaction and control when they can envision what is coming.

can show illustrations before ever reading the book together and give opportunities to make predictions, having children think about what might happen, why, why not, and so on. You can also use math manipulatives, blocks, or cards to create the beginning of various patterns and see if pairs of children can complete the sequence correctly. Children can do this for long periods of time, and they will enjoy a wide variety of pattern-detection games.

⚡ 18. Understand why television viewing is not OK for infants and toddlers.

How will knowing this help me?

Regardless of whether you are providing center-based care or home-based care, children under the age of two need the stimulation of human contact to wire their brains optimally. Why?

Television talk goes by too rapidly for the young developing brain. The sounds of language pass by quickly, and the child cannot slow the pace for better processing. A human, however, naturally modifies and modulates speech used with children. This happens almost by instinct. Because we love to look at babies and watch them carefully, we notice that they tune in when we talk using what is now called *parentese*. With very young babies, most adults around the world automatically raise the pitch of their voice, give more emphasis to long vowel sounds, and slow down their speech. It is wonderful to learn that this slower, higher-pitched, elongated speech matches up perfectly with the processing capabilities of an infant! Magic, right?

Study after study shows that for infants and toddlers to learn language, they must be able to see language produced. They need to watch—up close and personal—your lips, your teeth, and your tongue to really learn how to produce speech sounds.

BRAIN NUGGET

The American Academy of Pediatrics provides guidance encouraging parents to manage interactive screen time for their young children while continuing to limit passive television viewing for children under two years of age.

Observe children at this age as you talk to them, and you will notice that they are really studying your mouth. They sometimes even put their fingers into your mouth as you talk to feel how you do what you do! This process is indeed wonderful.

Sometimes parents will say that their child seems to be very engaged when watching the TV. Scientists now know that very young children do not truly comprehend the content from what is now referred to as passive television viewing; they are simply drawn to the movement of the constantly changing images. As noted in Brain Basics 101, the brain is naturally drawn to watching moving objects. Instead of TV, let the little ones watch pets or people who move. Young children are good at making us pay attention to them, and they enjoy paying attention to what adults are doing as well.

Very young children watch adults carefully and naturally imitate us, including how we use various technologies. Media capabilities are changing and growing rapidly. Interactive technologies that allow a child to make choices and receive immediate feedback and that promote decision making are different from classic TV watching. Research is ongoing to determine the effects of such technologies. The American Academy of Pediatrics (AAP) offers new guidelines as research informs new recommendations.

After age three and certainly by age five, children can learn effectively from television programming, research shows. The major circuitry in their brains has been connected, they typically have good command of the language, and they are interested in the content of what they watch. Be sure, therefore, that the content is appropriate for them to learn. Use your own common sense about what is good for a child.

So what should I try to do?

- In center-based care, remove televisions from the infant and toddler rooms. If you are providing in-home care, keep the television off while caring for young children. Parents are paying your center to provide state-of-the-art care, so you should abide by the recommendations from the AAP as they evolve. In Arizona, leaders have taken to heart this important recommendation about no passive television for children under age two. Understanding the distinction between classrooms for infants and toddlers and those for older children, the Arizona Department of Health mandated that, as a condition of licensure, all televisions be removed from classrooms caring for children under age two. This one act has the power to dramatically improve the interaction patterns among caregivers and children in every such classroom throughout the state. This environment allows caregivers to form stronger relationships with children, share more language, and get to know the children better.

- Do the same TV rules apply for parents and grandparents caring for their own children? No, there are no rules to enforce this recommendation, of course. Home settings often have different standards, and rightly so. But the science shows that, in general, families should avoid having their own children, especially infants, sitting in front of TVs.

Resources

American Academy of Pediatrics. 2015. "Media and Children." *American Academy of Pediatrics*, accessed September 17, 2015. https://www.aap.org/en-us /advocacy-and-policy/aap-health-initiatives/Pages/Media-and-Children.aspx

Christakis, Dimitri A., et al. 2004. "Early Television Exposure and Subsequent Attentional Problems in Children." *Pediatrics* 113(4): 708 –713.

Zull, James E. 2011. *From Brain to Mind: Using Neuroscience to Guide Change in Education.* Sterling, VA: Stylus Publishing.

⚡ 19. Understand the importance of face time.

How will knowing this help me?

At birth, infants' vision is clearest at a distance of about 8 to 10 inches. When a baby is nursing at the breast or sucking from a bottle, this is approximately the distance between the infant's eyes and the caregiver's face. Incredibly interesting, isn't it?

So right from the start, babies pay attention to faces. Infants react to changes in a face by the age of one to three months. Studies show that babies prefer to look at faces longer than any other image. By looking at your face while you talk slowly to them and by studying the movements of your teeth, tongue, and lips, babies learn to mimic those same movements. This imitation is important to their efforts to coordinate the muscle groups needed to progress from making babbling sounds to producing language.

You provide the model; you are a key source of how to produce language. That is why being close enough to study the model is so important! As noted before, babies and young toddlers will even put their fingers into your mouth as you talk to feel how you make the sounds. Remember that in the multisensory world of a young child, seeing, hearing, and touching work together to mentally map the learning of a new skill.

So what should I try to do?

- Stay up close when talking to a child of any age. Even though the visual range and skills increase rapidly as a child reaches about six months of age, seeing your face will continue to help the child imitate your language production.

> **BRAIN NUGGET**
>
> Face time (up close and personal) allows children to learn language. They need to be able to watch your teeth, your tongue, and your lips to see how language is produced.

- Encourage young children to watch themselves in the mirror, as they are fascinated by their own movements. Lay the infant on his tummy to explore his reflection in a nearby, safe mirror. As the infant attends to the face in the mirror, you can promote development by building up tummy time.

⚡ 20. Be intentional about increasing the child's attention span.

How will knowing this help me?

Several factors are known to capture human attention. These include emotion, size, personal significance, novelty, intensity, and incongruity. Intensity, for example, refers to great energy, concentration, or strength. In practice, you might show it by speaking in a very loud or very soft voice, using an object with a concentration of color, or expressing enthusiasm.

Caregivers can use these different factors to help capture and maintain a child's attention. When reading, for example, you can show your enthusiasm by modulating your voice to show excitement. Eye contact is also critical to gaining someone's attention. Emotionally engaging facial expressions, along with voice inflections, help to capture attention. Children will attend to the book or the task for longer and longer periods of time when captivated by you!

BRAIN NUGGET

Talking or reading to a child with great interest and enthusiasm about the story's pictures or ideas can increase the attention span.

So what should I try to do?

- Gain attention through eye contact. A child needs to realize that you are connecting with her deliberately. Establishing eye contact is a clear signal of your intent.

- Once eye contact is secure, point to pictures or objects that you want a child to focus on. *Shared gaze* is a term used to indicate that you and the child are focused on the same thing at the same time. Enthusiasm is again important in this transition from initial eye contact to a shared gaze of looking together at something else.

- Adjusting your pace of reading or talking can help to maintain attention. The brain is primed to react to change, so use this to your advantage.

- Involve the child in the story by occasionally asking questions that require her to pay attention.

- Attention span increases over time with practice and age, so do not be disheartened when at first a child might not pay attention for as long as you would like. You do not need to push beyond the point where you and the child are having fun. Short sessions of focused attention will gradually expand for longer and longer periods of enjoyment.

⚡ 21. Simplify the classroom or care environment to be visually soothing.

How will knowing this help me?

For many years, traditional early childhood environments have been created using wildly colorful paints, primary-colored and bold drawings, colorful objects hanging everywhere, and many toys and books scattered on floors, with overflowing cupboards and shelves. Stimulating? Yes. Overstimulating? Perhaps. A young child's brain can easily become overstimulated by too many competing elements.

In the first fourteen months of an infant's life, the brain is rapidly wiring up to learn to pay attention. There are three different brain regions that wire for attention, each area contributing different aspects of the entire circuitry needed to be able to capture, shift, and maintain attention. The brain regions used for alerting (capturing attention) and for orienting (switching attention) tend to make the necessary connections almost completely by fourteen months. The last regions, used for maintaining and sustaining attention, create the needed connections by about age seven. What this really means is that the attention system in the human brain is formed early.

Although the attention system wires early, it also is changeable and malleable. This means that experiences can influence the development of the system. The strategies used to care for and educate young children can positively or negatively affect these developing brain regions. So, too, perhaps can the physical environment.

So what should I try to do?

Think about what it means to have a soothing environment. Think about the word *soothe* itself, which means "to gently calm someone." Synonyms include *calm down, comfort, quiet, settle down, ease, relieve,* and *take the edge off.* It is true that children, because they are so actively exploring their environment, need lots of opportunities to be stimulated and excited.

But children also need times and spaces that are not typically defined in terms of stimulation. They can also benefit by the efforts caregivers make to soothe them during the day. One way you can do this is by fostering a balance of active and quiet learning. Create environments that promote safe exploration where children can expand their knowledge and mastery of their world.

- Look for ways to remove clutter. Develop places and spaces for children and caregivers to find and use materials and then put them away.

- Reduce the chaos. Choose routines that bring order and predictability. Overly exciting experiences need to be counterbalanced with predictably calming times and spaces.

BRAIN NUGGET

Visually calming environments can diffuse overstimulation and encourage children to have more focused attention.

- Try neutral backgrounds for walls and spaces. If possible, infuse the environment with natural light, and add nontoxic, easy-to-maintain live plants. These elements can give the space a calming and soothing look and feel.

- Circulate toys and books to keep children's interest high in new things they can explore. That way, you can avoid having too many things that then detract from a child's ability to find something truly captivating!

- Create environments that promote touching, observing, listening, and moving. Each type of experience requires that you plan ways to have these experiences available at times throughout the day. Some preschool environments manage this through learning centers for language learning, math and manipulatives, arts, sensory exploration, and dramatic play.

⚡ 22. Provide lots of practice for children to begin to learn impulse control.

How will knowing this help me?

What we commonly call *impulse control* requires many systems in the brain to work together to inhibit or stop an action. Stopping an action is one of the hardest things that a developing brain needs to learn how to do. In the brain, it is easier to initiate movement and action than it is to stop it. Recognizing this fact may help adults begin to understand why children need lots of help controlling their behavior.

As soon as a child learns an action, she has a tendency to more easily repeat the action in similar circumstances in the future. That, in most cases, is good news. The brain starts to perform many actions, almost automatically. It works fine until you want a child to stop doing something; that is hard in many cases. Often, overflow actions occur before stopping is accomplished. When a child starts to run and then begins to stop, it can take a few extra seconds before she completely stops.

BRAIN NUGGET

Impulse control begins slowly and is not easy to achieve. It is nevertheless a goal that teachers and parents work toward for years with every child.

If you now add strong desire—such as "I really want this cookie" or "This toy is mine"—you see that voluntary control is even more difficult. When a child has trust in a responsible adult, she can more successfully delay gratification of something she really wants. Being a reliable adult is critical because children can more easily manage their impulses when they believe that their needs and wants actually will be satisfied after the wait. They will have the confidence that if they do delay immediate gratification, then the wait can be worth it.

So what should I try to do?

- For an enjoyable experience, watch a YouTube video called "The Marshmallow Test." One of the best versions was filmed in September 2009 (www.youtube .com/watch?v=QX_oy9614HQ). This funny video depicts a now-classic research study that looked at how long typical five-year-olds can delay the impulse to eat a wonderful-smelling marshmallow when they are left alone to wait with the tempting treat sitting in front of them. This will help you understand just how difficult it is to delay gratification—especially when a child is so young. Note the very clever distraction techniques! Some of the little ones will sit on their hands or turn completely around so that they can't see the treat. Others pick up the marshmallow and smell it before pushing the temptation away. Enjoy watching these children as they try to resist!

- Provide practice in stopping movement by playing some fun and easy games such as Red Light, Green Light, which requires children to stop moving when the leader calls out "red light"; or Statue, which requires children to freeze and hold their positions like statues on the leader's command.

- Play the popular game Simon Says. Children are naturally inclined to respond to the leader's directions of taking a particular action, but they must try to resist if the command does not begin with the specific words *Simon says*.

- Be sure to keep a promise if you have asked a child to temporarily give up what she wants or to wait for what she needs by telling her that she will get it later. Be sure that *later* does come, and it should come faster for very young children.

- For toddlers and preschoolers, spend time talking about and illustrating emotions that all children naturally have. Children get angry. Adults get angry. Begin to demonstrate that the child can have a feeling without needing to act on it.

- Add a step to your own habit of giving children directions. After verbalizing what you want them to do and not do, have them repeat what they have heard before they launch off to begin. This important step, once it becomes a habit, begins to teach children how to listen instead of merely hearing.

- When children know they are safe, their brains are able save some energy. They use this energy savings (that they might have used to monitor their own well-being) for learning new concepts. They are then able to focus some of their energy on their own talents and preferences. Learning about themselves in their current environment can begin to help them better regulate their behavior and emotions.

- Be careful to limit the amount of time you ask children to sit and focus. Fidgety children who have been sitting too long begin to lose their self-control.

- Allow for sufficient imaginative-play opportunities. Children can work out their frustrations by dressing up as characters and making up rules that apply to actual challenges they have encountered. Sometimes dramatic play allows them to tackle problems that seem too monumental in real life.

- Self-speak is another good way for a child to slow down and talk through a problem before acting it out. A think-aloud can guide a child to make a good choice. Adults do this all the time in a subvocalized way when we tell ourselves to take a breath, slow down, or give it a rest.

⚡ 23. Provide stable, consistent, and challenging environments that encourage children to develop the foundation of executive functions in the brain.

How will knowing this help me?

A particular set of cognitive skills called *executive functions* actually consists of thinking skills that have their origins in early childhood. It is an umbrella term for the neurologically based skills involving mental control and self-regulation.

Because one aspect of the brain-development sequence is from the back to the front, the last regions to develop fully are the frontal lobes. The frontal lobes are responsible for abstract reasoning, planning, understanding the consequences of one's behavior, impulse control, prioritizing, and orchestrating the action plans necessary to solve problems. Skills also include monitoring, evaluating, and adapting different strategies to accomplish different tasks, as well as the ability to analyze situations, focus and maintain attention, and adjust actions as needed to get the job done. Clearly, these are high-level thinking skills that are necessary to operate in a complex society, to earn a living, to raise children, and to compete in the economy. These skills, although they develop slowly over time, have their roots in early childhood experiences that provide practice in these skills.

Practice is key. As a caregiver, strive to provide lots of opportunities for children to exercise their frontal lobes. Because these brain regions are not yet fully developed, do not expect consistently high performance of these complex skills. However, you can support a child's efforts to begin thinking about why he wants to do something, set a goal based on that idea, organize small tasks that will help him achieve that goal, and then strive to carry them out. As children practice these skills over and over, they get better at them! Realize that there will be failures, incomplete tries, and maybe even some meltdowns when things don't work out. But this learning by trial and error can help children move toward better thinking. The key is to provide scaffolding—providing temporary support while a child learns and takes steps toward accomplishing a task on his own—and enthusiastically support these early attempts.

BRAIN NUGGET

Executive functions include important thinking and planning skills that develop throughout childhood, adolescence, and early adulthood, and allow mature adults to perform at their highest levels of competence.

So what should I try to do?

- If you are providing care for infants, the basic attention, bonding, and communication routines you already use are encouraging the unfolding of healthy brain development. The mindful use of these processes and procedures will ensure that the infants' needs are met in loving, predictable ways.

- If you work with young toddlers, you can begin to teach how to organize a day using routines. Providing structure gives a toddler's brain practice in knowing what happens first, next, and last. Think of actions your children take every day, and then highlight aspects of those very ordinary actions that are tied to a goal. Next, highlight the steps you take to accomplish that goal. Finish by noting that the goal has been reached. Be explicit. Labeling how things get accomplished helps the frontal lobes begin understanding patterns and logical-thinking processes.

- If you work with older toddlers, let them begin to set simple goals. Watch out though! A child may launch into a wild and extravagant goal such as taking a trip to Disneyland! Start by giving children choices between two possible goals. Walk them through the steps they need to think about to reach their goals. Monitor their progress, continually providing scaffolding and giving feedback.

- If you work with preschoolers, you can add more-complex tasks that require an organized plan. For example, you might have the children follow the steps in a recipe. Giving children opportunities to practice tasks in similar step-by-step ways can be fun and intellectually challenging while promoting connections in the frontal lobes.

PART 5
Bonding Messages

⚡ 24. Realize the power of having at least one consistent person who loves you.

How will knowing this help me?

Although there are many things that contribute to the healthy unfolding of a new human brain, neuroscientists have now confirmed what many wonderful teachers and parents have always instinctively known: the most important thing a child needs is at least one person who loves him, one person who can be counted on to always be present and loving, one person who will never give up on that child!

A child can certainly have more than one person, but what matters most is that there is at least that one person who is consistently and responsively there. If a child is lucky, that one person is her parent. However, if a parent is not available, then a grandparent, a foster parent, and yes, even a consistent teacher or caregiver will do just fine. The key is that the loving, responsive care is coming from the same person, over time.

BRAIN NUGGET

A strong bond to at least one loving, predictable, responsive caregiver is the most important factor in creating a healthy brain.

So what should I try to do?

Look at your situation.

- If you are a center director, know that you should make every effort to keep the same caregiver with the same child for as long as possible. Read about what is called *continuity of care* in the field. The Zero to Three website defines this term as follows: "Continuity of care means that children and caregivers remain together for more than one year, often for the first three years of the child's life. It can take different forms." (http://www.zerotothree.org/early-care-education /child-care/primary-caregiving-continuity.html) One option is for a caregiver to move to older classrooms as the children do. Another possibility is to have the children start as infants in a mixed-age group and remain with the same caregiver for several years until they are the oldest and move on.

- If you operate an in-home child care business, you are in a great position to maintain healthy long-term relationships with the children in your care. Once again, read about the concept of continuity of care, and be able to articulate what it is and why it matters to your families. Highlight this approach as one of the advantages a family should know about. It is a business asset you can advertise!

- If you are a caregiver or an early childhood teacher in an established child care company, try to influence your team and your management to keep children with a secure primary caregiver as much as possible. Experiment with ways to organize staffing patterns to allow for this. Consistency and continuity of caregiving for the birth-to-three population should become a primary goal of teaching staff.

Resources:

Shonkoff, Jack P., and Deborah A. Phillips, eds. 2000. *From Neurons to Neighborhoods: The Science of Early Childhood Development*. Washington, DC: National Academies Press.

Theilheimer, Rachel. 2006. "Primary Caregiving and Continuity of Care." Excerpted from "Molding to the Children: Primary Caregiving and Continuity of Care." *Zero to Three* 26(3): 50–54. http://www.zerotothree.org/early-care-education/ child-care/primary-caregiving-continuity.html

⚡ 25. Respond rapidly to the needs of infants.

How will knowing this help me?

The brain structures required for a baby to purposefully manipulate an adult simply are not present yet in the infant brain. Again, knowing your Brain Basics 101 reminds you that two of the four ways that the baby's brain develops are from the back to the front and from the inside out. The following information helps explain why this is true.

Because development occurs from the inside out, the structures of the limbic system in the centermost regions, where emotional processing occurs, are already active in infants. When babies cry, it is because they need something. However, they may not yet know how to express what that need is. When caregivers respond to babies quickly and predictably and meet those needs, the infants are soothed. The brain starts to recognize this pattern, and the child learns not to worry because discomfort will end and comfort will come. By responding consistently, you are building trust.

Early learning occurs through association. The younger the child, the more basic the associative connection. Several things happen when caregivers respond quickly and predictably to infants. First, infants learn that when they are distressed, someone will help them. This important link can actually lessen the crying and fussing babies might do, because they have learned that help is on its way! They can begin to calm themselves because they know that if they are hungry, they will be fed. If they are tired, they will have help going to sleep. If they are wet, they will be changed and will feel more comfortable. Second, children form an emotional association between the sight, sound, and smell of the caregiver and the sense of satisfaction that will follow. This positive association is linked to the beginning of the love relationship.

As the brain develops from the back to the front, the visual cortex at the back makes connections rapidly as the infant visually processes the people and objects he sees. However, the frontal lobes where planning,

> **BRAIN NUGGET**
>
> You cannot spoil an infant by attending to him quickly when he needs something.

organizing, and strategizing are located are barely active at birth. These frontal areas develop slowly over time, continuing into early adulthood. The neural development needed to plan how to get the attention of a relative or another caregiver is not complete, and the baby is not yet capable of manipulation.

Yet is a key word. Can you spoil a two-year-old? You bet you can.

In the first two years, the brain has been rapidly forming neural networks in the toddler's frontal lobe. Young children experiment with cause and effect. Toddlers are certainly capable of throwing themselves to the ground in a tantrum because they want something—just because they want it! Caregivers slowly begin the process of teaching (the best form of disciplining) what children can and cannot have at the moment they want something. The use of *external regulation* starts forming predictable patterns that lead a child toward *internal self-regulation*. The boundaries you set and the rules you create to keep a two-year-old safe are examples of new patterns that a child's brain will learn through repetition.

So what should I try to do?

- Pay close attention to the earliest signs of communication from an infant. When possible, catch the first moment when a baby starts to fuss, typically before he starts to cry. Respond. Verbally letting an infant know that you are coming can become linked to the reduction in his distress. Always soothe in calm and consistent ways.

- Over time, learn the differences in the infant's cries associated with hunger versus boredom versus overstimulation. Because the brain is a pattern-seeking organ, you and the baby can both find meaning in the messages you send back and forth.

- Set reasonable limits for toddlers. You will likely have to remind them countless times about what they can and cannot do. Repeatedly setting limits in a calm way is the key to learning and maintaining the integrity of the trust relationship.

⚡ 26. Touch to calm; touch for better health.

How will knowing this help me?

Genuine affection, as shown through loving touch, can influence both cognitive and social-emotional development.

Studies at the Touch Research Institute at the University of Miami have shown many benefits of gentle massage for children and for adults as well:

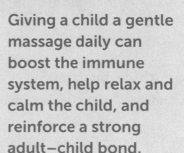

BRAIN NUGGET

Giving a child a gentle massage daily can boost the immune system, help relax and calm the child, and reinforce a strong adult–child bond.

- Greater weight gains in premature infants, resulting in earlier hospital discharge and, therefore, tangible health and economic benefits

- Less anxiousness, deeper sleep, and more alert states reported for six-month-olds

- Enhanced attentiveness in toddlers and preschoolers

- Reduction in the stress hormone cortisol in children and adults

- Reduction in blood pressure in children and adults

- Improved immune functions in all groups tested against controls

Tiffany Field of the Touch Research Institute cites research that massage and soothing touch can comfort children, increase their sense of security, and reaffirm close bonds with them. In addition, a study by researcher Justin Crane and colleagues found that massage can "turn off genes associated with inflammation and turn on genes that help muscles heal" (https://newsinhealth.nih.gov/issue/jul2012/feature2).

So what should I try to do?

The research on the power of touch is mounting, but caregivers face a challenge understanding when and where they can appropriately use it.

- With your own children, infant and toddler massage at bath or bedtime is appropriate.

- In center-based or in-home care, the more appropriate kinds of touch that operate on the same principles include comfort touch, caring touch, and gentle holding, all of which can lower the stress hormone cortisol. A warm touch can also release and increase oxytocin, a hormone associated with increased feelings of comfort and trust. These easy and natural forms of touch have been shown to do the following:

  - Allow heart rate and breathing to slow down and regulate

  - Reduce blood pressure and stress hormones

  - Increase pain-killing endorphins

  - Boost the immune system

- With preschoolers, try a high five. Even that touch connection signals "nice job," "I like it," or "I agree with you," and it does so without words!

- With older children, a teacher's supportive touch on the back or arm can result in better attention and increased participation in class.

If you are interested in a deeper understanding of the power of massage for young children and why touch triggers a cascade of positive events in the body, consider consulting some of the resources listed here.

Resources

Crane, Justin D., et al. 2012. "Massage Therapy Attenuates Inflammatory Signaling After Exercise-Induced Muscle Damage." *Science Translational Medicine* 4(119). http://stm.sciencemag.org/content/4/119/119ra13

Field, Tiffany. 2001. *Touch.* Cambridge, MA: Massachusetts Institute of Technology.

Heath, Alan., and Nicki Bainbridge. 2004. *Baby Massage: The Calming Power of Touch.* New York: DK Publishing.

National Institutes of Health. 2012. "Massage Therapy: What You Knead to Know." *NIH News in Health.* https://newsinhealth.nih.gov/issue/jul2012/feature2

Reese, Suzanne P. 2006. *Baby Massage: Soothing Strokes for Healthy Growth.* London: Viking Studio.

Touch Research Institute. 2016. "Research at TRI." *Touch Research Institute*, accessed January 11, 2016. http://www6.miami.edu/touch-research/Research.html

⚡ 27. Hold children close so they know they are secure.

How will knowing this help me?

A child loves the feeling of your body warmth and your breath on his head

because it is so comforting and soothing. This feeling of connection allows a child to feel safe and secure. Feeling secure is critical for healthy brain development. By repeating this soothing experience regularly, a caregiver builds trust, and the child begins to associate his caregiver with a sense of feeling safe.

As you know from Brain Basics 101, the drive for survival is universal. When repeated experiences teach a child to trust that safety is assured, the brain's energy is free to focus on many other things.

So what should I try to do?

- Be mindful of creating multiple opportunities for a child to be physically close to you. This can be done easily by holding a baby, toddler, or preschooler in your lap as you read a book together. Think about this idea of your breath on his head. Think of other ways to allow a child to feel your closeness. Gently stroke his arm as you discuss the pictures and the story together. Run your fingers through his hair. Relax the tension in your own body, and see if you can feel that same responsive release in the child.

- Rock a child to comfort him and you. Gentle motion is known to relax us all. Hum or sing softly to a child as you hold him close. The child will be able to feel the vibration of your humming. What a soothing balm that can be!

- Knowing that you are safe at all times is important to adults, but it is critical to the healthy unfolding of a brain for infants, toddlers, preschoolers, and older children. When a child does not feel safe, the primal fight-or-flight region of the brain takes over and consumes energy that could otherwise be used for learning. In a high-stress situation where a child's sense of security is threatened, the first responsibility of the adult is to regain and reestablish a safe environment.

BRAIN NUGGET

Hold a young child close as often as you can. This physical closeness allows a child to feel and enjoy the warmth of your breath on his head. Close physical contact also contributes to a child's sense of safety, which is critical to healthy cognitive development as well as social-emotional health.

⚡ 28. Express your genuine love and respect daily to those in your care.

How will knowing this help me?

Children's brains develop optimally when safety, love, and comfort are ever present. If you think back to several of the notions developed in the Brain Basics 101 section, you can begin to see why this is true.

The limbic system—containing central structures in the brain that process emotions, regulate responses to stimuli, and monitor the surroundings for threats—develops in response to qualities in the immediate environment that dominate. Negative, stressful, and chaotic homes and classrooms can increase hypervigilance (always worrying that something hurtful could happen) and contribute not only to aggressive behaviors but also to impulsive, dysregulated emotions. Positive, comforting, and secure homes and classrooms, where positive emotions and love are the norm and dominate, lead to better self-regulation and more positive self-concepts in young children.

Possibly lifelong patterns of behavior and self-image are developed in part by what children see and hear in these earliest years: "I love you!" "You are so funny!" "What a cool tower you built!" "You are the hardest worker I can imagine." "I love your laugh!" If you accompany the positive words with hugs, winks, and smiles, you will build stronger, more successful children.

So what should I try to do?

- If you are a center director, hire positive people who are not embarrassed that they love people. Check references carefully, and seek feedback that will tell you about a person's capacity to stay positive and to authentically show love. Use positive reinforcement yourself in

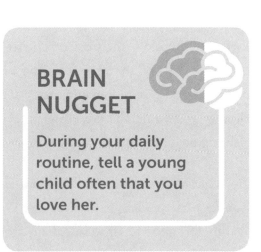

BRAIN NUGGET

During your daily routine, tell a young child often that you love her.

your evaluations and interactions with staff. Do not be afraid to express gratitude for the wonderful things you observe caregivers doing. Be specific in noticing what they do well, with an especially exuberant response when you see a caregiver fall in love with a child.

- If you are a caregiver in a home or center, create environments that allow children to feel safe and to know they are loved and cared for. Next, show your love, affection, and caring to each child multiple times each day. The old adage "actions speak louder than words" is of course true. But when it comes to loving feelings, psychologists and mental-health professionals are learning that it also matters that people hear the words of loving and caring, as Daniel Siegel notes in his book *The Developing Mind*. Many adults report with some degree of sadness that they grew up never hearing, "I love you," or similar positive messages. Being told that you are loved, that you try so hard when you are striving for something, or that you are really missed when you are absent are verbal messages that can last a lifetime.

Resources

Siegel, Daniel J. 1999. *The Developing Mind: Toward a Neurobiology of Interpersonal Experience.* New York: Guilford Press.

⚡ 29. Enjoy the practice of reading to children.

How will knowing this help me?

Little children love the total experience of having you read to them. Eventually, they recognize that you are taking time to focus your attention on them. Regardless of which book you choose, children note that you are sitting calmly holding one or more of them close to you while you are lilting your voice with expression and talking with them, elaborating a bit, smiling, and telling stories.

This kind of attention just feels good, so the brain says, "Wow, let's do that again." No wonder early reading is so powerful! Wouldn't that same level of calm attention and sharing feel good to any of us, at any age?

So what should I try to do?

- Set up your day to have short but frequent times that you slow down, sit down, and read with one or more children. Keep many books handy, especially core books, which can be read over and over any time of the year.

- Circulate and change out your selection, but recycle favorites back into the sequence. Children love the familiar. In fact, most of us love the familiar, and that is because the brain recognizes repeated stories, or repeated anything, as something that is already safe and something that we can therefore relax about. It may seem odd, but while every brain searches for the novel stimulus, the brain still appreciates and is comforted by the familiar as well.

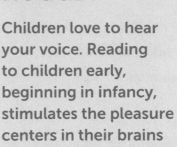

BRAIN NUGGET

Children love to hear your voice. Reading to children early, beginning in infancy, stimulates the pleasure centers in their brains and strengthens the caregiver–child bond.

⚡ 30. Promote touch through guided exploration of common experiences.

How will knowing this help me?

Living in a "Don't touch!" world may temporarily keep order and occasionally promote safety but more often deprives children of important understandings that are best learned through touch.

To begin to form concepts, a child must first figure out if there is any matching idea already in her brain. This is called *prior knowledge*. In the area of touch, concept development occurs as the child explores and determines if a new sensation is the same or different from what she already knows.

For example, if a child has experienced hot water and now feels a hot towel as it is removed from the clothes dryer, the concept of *hot* is quickly extended to include both water and things coming freshly from the dryer. This concept elaboration is confirmed when you, the caregiver, label that feeling as hot. Of course you would be sure not to let a child touch something that is so hot it is dangerous! The child builds contrasting concepts rapidly by testing each and every thing in the environment to confirm, extend, or find something that doesn't fit. Educators sometimes refer to these processes as *assimilation*, which involves adding examples to a concept, and *accommodation*, which involves modifying a prior idea.

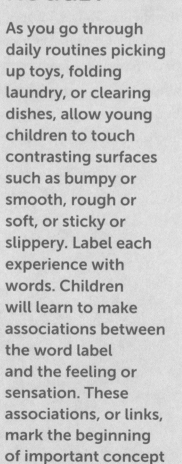

BRAIN NUGGET

As you go through daily routines picking up toys, folding laundry, or clearing dishes, allow young children to touch contrasting surfaces such as bumpy or smooth, rough or soft, or sticky or slippery. Label each experience with words. Children will learn to make associations between the word label and the feeling or sensation. These associations, or links, mark the beginning of important concept development.

Introducing sensations with high contrast is a good starting point for this type of concept development.

So what should I try to do?

- Under your guidance and supervision, allow children to reach out and explore objects and environments as they begin to learn how things work. Comment on how things are the same or different. Start with simple contrasting concepts such as bumpy and smooth.

- Extend children's hands-on experiences and begin talking about the many new ideas that can be seen in children's books that add visual contrasts, such as shiny and dull, striped and spotted, or sparkly and plain.

- As children become more sophisticated in their reading, add contrasting emotional labels such as grumpy and jolly, and stern and gentle. Playing a game of opposites can be a fun challenge for preschoolers, and building the concepts that support these contrasts can start early through the sensation of touch.

⚡ 31. Show photos of key people to a child to build a sense of security.

How will knowing this help me?

The brain of a young child pays particular attention to visual stimuli. The visual system wires up early, and early learnings are powerful. Because young children learn most things first by seeing, be visual when you share information in your classroom or learning environment. Post pictures of things you want children to learn. Show first, before you tell.

Clear, realistic photos are especially easy for a preschooler or toddler to attend to. Reviewing photos of parents, grandparents, siblings, and other regular caregivers can help children feel connected to people who love them.

So what should I try to do?

- After making a small photo album of loved ones for each child, sit and review the photos often with the child.

- With younger children, use simple, clear photos of loved ones' faces. As children get older, they can handle typical family photos that include groups of people at a slightly more distant view.

- Talk about each person as you show the photos. Remind the child how much he is loved. Include stories you have learned about each person pictured in the album. Stories and facts that can be shared can be noted on the back of each page. These stories can be discovered by talking to the child's family member who provided the photos.

- Find or draw pictures of procedures and routines you want children to follow and use them to explain and reinforce your expectations. Children will more easily learn what to do from seeing a picture than from hearing directions.

> **BRAIN NUGGET**
>
> Make small books of family or classmate photos to share with each child frequently. This helps a child feel connected to the key people in his world, strengthening a sense of security and confidence.

⚡ 32. Teach first in the language of the heart when encouraging dual-language development.

How will knowing this help me?

Research shows that very young children can easily learn two languages at the same time. If a family member speaks a second language, it is fine to have both languages spoken to the young child. Brain scans of young bilingual children show that the same language regions in the brain are used to process both languages.

Young bilingual children learn best when one family member speaks to them in his native language (for example, Spanish) and another family member speaks in her native language that is different (perhaps English). The child can learn the vocabulary, grammar, syntax, and pronunciations of each language correctly. Young children can easily code-switch between languages when needed.

In the United States today, many children live in homes where a language other than English is the primary language. Parents who are native speakers of another language sometimes mistakenly decide to speak very little to their young children at home for fear that it will hurt their children's ability to learn English later. Experiencing very little talk in the homes, the children can become language deprived. Parents should know that toddlers and preschoolers can easily and successfully add a second language if they have a strong foundation in their first language. Parents will be relieved to discover that they should talk, read, and sing in their native language so that their child's brain develops fluency first in that language. The richness of the language experience can occur in that native language, and then the child has a competent base from which she can learn a second language—which could be English or another language.

Learning to speak two languages does not delay language development. Researcher Fred Genesee has noted that according to test results, bilingual and monolingual children reach critical milestones at the same ages (typical time periods when a child speaks one word, two words, short sentences, and so on).

BRAIN NUGGET

Encourage the use and development of more than one language, but teach first in the language in which you would say "I love you" to the child. Meaningful exposure to a second language from an early age can greatly benefit a child's cognitive development and social-emotional well-being. Bilingual children can learn and maintain two languages easily without loss in either language.

In addition, there is important new evidence that fluent young bilingual children can develop great cognitive benefits, especially in the critically important frontal lobes. (See Brain Basics 101 for more on frontal-lobe functions.) *Code switching*, often occurring when translating from one language to another, brings more activation to the frontal-lobe regions. The increased use of these regions brings more nutrients and blood flow to the areas and results in earlier and better development of the frontal lobes. More mature frontal lobes result in the following:

- Better ability to focus

- Increased ability to filter out distractions—resulting in more inhibitory control, which is the ability to ignore competing information while continuing to focus on a task

- Increased cognitive reserve, which means denser neural development that can last into adulthood, thus delaying mental deterioration in old age

So what should I try to do?

- If you are caring for other people's children, be sure to clarify whether the parents are interested in having their child learn another language. If you speak more than one language, expose the children to the sounds, vocabulary, and pronunciations of both languages.

- If you have parental permission, or if you are a parent taking care of your own child at home, talk, talk, talk all day to the infant or toddler in your native language to ensure strong language skills. A second language can be learned simultaneously or added at any time during early childhood with great ease. Even hearing different language sounds helps keep those sounds active in a child's brain.

- There are now many bilingual books that you can read to young children that reinforce the fact that there can be two or more words in different languages to label one object or to express an idea. The continued development of this kind of cognitive flexibility is an asset later in life.

- Throughout the United States, there are growing numbers of children's television programs in both English and Spanish. Although pediatricians do not recommend that infants and young toddlers watch television, children ages four and five can enjoy watching and listening to these shows with you. The best approach is to then discuss the ideas and new words with a child to extend her comprehension abilities.

- Try sharing children's songs and rhymes in a variety of languages so that all children in a group setting can learn them. This helps develop an appreciation for other languages.

- Share this important information with parents you know. Be sure to emphasize the significance of having rich language experiences in one's native language. It is important to realize that bilingual ability is an asset to be developed and valued.

Resources

Bialystok, Ellen, Fergus I. M. Craik, and Gigi Luk. 2012. "Bilingualism: Consequences for Mind and Brain." *Trends in Cognitive Sciences* 16(4): 240–250.

Bialystok, Ellen, and Michelle M. Martin. 2004. "Attention and Inhibition in Bilingual Children: Evidence from the Dimensional Change Card Sort Task." *Developmental Science* 7(3): 325–339.

Genesee, Fred. 2008. "Early Dual Language Learning," *Zero to Three* 29(1): 17–23.

Hernandez, Arturo E., Antigona Martinez, and Kathryn Kohnert. 2000. "In Search of the Language Switch: An fMRI Study of Picture Naming in Spanish–English Bilinguals." *Brain and Language* 73(3): 421–431.

⚡ 33. Use music to help bond with young children.

How will knowing this help me?

Music is a natural, enjoyable part of the environment, especially for young children. Music brings feelings of joy that can be shared with others and that can serve to connect people. Providing a variety of music experiences (including singing to and with children and playing simple instruments) at different times in the day can be advantageous to early child development.

As caregivers of young children, there are a number of findings that should encourage the introduction of music in many forms into early childhood settings. There are also several myths that should be clarified. One such myth is that just listening to classical music will make a child smarter. Such assertions, though probably well intentioned, have caused confusion and some mistrust of the benefits of music for young children.

Here are some important findings:

- There is little scientific evidence that just listening to classical music can change or enhance brain structures. However, growing evidence shows that learning to play a musical instrument at a very young age (particularly the violin or the piano) does tend to positively influence brain development, especially in some regions of the brain associated with learning math and science concepts.

> **BRAIN NUGGET**
>
> Research shows that frequent music involvement, such as listening to music, singing rhymes and songs, and playing musical instruments and keyboards, can be important to later emotional and intellectual development.

- There is evidence that early music exposure, especially to experiences that teach a child how to keep a steady beat with the music, can make learning to read easier. When children are actively engaged with simple musical instruments—such as maracas and tambourines—and focus on the tempo of the music, they are learning to detect patterns and to improve their attention skills.

- Musical engagement can also improve auditory discrimination, which is the ability to hear small differences in sounds. This skill is, in turn, associated with better phonemic awareness, a part of preliteracy that is essential in learning to read. Such a focus on small changes in sound can lead to changes throughout the auditory system by making it more sensitive.

So what should I try to do?

- Sing together. Sing and listen to a variety of music, including classical music, of course! Also, chant some familiar rhymes in chorus.

- Dance together. Body movements, inspired by music, help young children learn to coordinate moving different parts of their bodies. Because it is difficult sometimes for children to know where their bodies are in space, try teaching very simple movements that can help regulate children's ability to consciously move parts of their bodies.

- Clap out the beat of many familiar songs, and add in a few new songs. If you have access to simple musical instruments such as maracas or bells, engage children in using these to keep the steady beat of the music. Active participation is key. Give each child a chance to use the materials.

- Use music in daily routines; it can help signal transitions between activities. Children begin to associate certain songs with upcoming, daily schedule changes such as cleanup time, nap time, play time, and lunch time.

- Avoid playing background music throughout the entire day. Many young children cannot filter out noise as easily as adults can. Too much background music may escalate the overall noise level as the day continues. Instead, use specific types of music to accomplish specific goals: transitioning from one activity to another, calming for quiet times, and changing the pace of the day when the energy becomes too high or low.

- Notice that some young children will use a song or parts of a tune to soothe themselves and to relax. They may hum or sing softly as they start to slow down and relax. This is a wonderful way for a child to learn to self-regulate, focus, and manage his own activity level.

Resources

Saffran, Jenny R. 2003. "Musical Learning and Language Development." *Annals of the New York Academy of Sciences* 999: 397–401.

Tallal, Paula, and Nadine Gaab. 2006. "Dynamic Auditory Processing, Musical Experience and Language Development." *Trends in Neurosciences* 29(7): 382–390.

Woodruff Carr, Kali, et al. 2014. "Beat Synchronization Predicts Neural Speech Encoding and Reading Readiness in Preschoolers." *Proceedings of the National Academy of Sciences, USA* 111(40): 14559–14564. http://www.pnas.org /content/111/40/14559.full.pdf

---

⚡ 34. Comment on a child's effort rather than on how smart a child is.

How will knowing this help me?

Children who are constantly told how smart they are, often even when the accomplishment may be minor, develop resistance to trying new things if they think they might fail at the first try. They want to maintain the idea of being smart and can shy away from any challenge that could threaten that image of themselves. If they try and do not succeed, they may view the outcome as a failure of who they are rather than recognize that the task may just have been very difficult or that it may take time and help to achieve.

Positive feedback and praise based on how much the child tried, regardless of whether the effort resulted in success, allows a child to realize that with more learning or practice, she can do the following:

- Try again

- Ask for suggestions or help from other children or adults

- Come back to the task later

- Decide that it is not something she is ready for yet

Stanford University researcher Carol Dweck has found that the mind-set one develops matters. Some people have a fixed mind-set, believing that their abilities are inborn and that these predetermined traits are responsible for their successes. Other people have a growth mind-set, believing that hard work, education, and tenacity are the basis for success. This growth mind-set tends to result in better long-term outcomes.

BRAIN NUGGET

Positive feedback helps children in many, many ways. However, research shows that it is best to praise children for their effort rather than to praise them for how intelligent they are.

So what should I try to do?

- With little ones, encourage them with comments such as, "Come on, you can do it . . . keep trying." "Nice job!" "Can I help you a little?"

- With toddlers, you might say, "Nice work! You were trying really hard." "I love it. You really gave it your all!"

- With preschoolers who are gaining more independence and pride in themselves, try statements such as, "You have figured that out really nicely. Is there anything you want to do differently?" "Keep going; you are making great progress. Let me know if you need my help. You can show me what you need me to do."

- At each stage of development, the motivation to keep going and to keep learning sets up brain responses that activate the brain's reward system. Physiological pleasure becomes linked to the feelings of learning and effort. Thus begins the very important development of positive self-esteem and internal motivation.

Resources
Dweck, Carol. 2007. *Mindset: The New Psychology of Success.* New York: Random House.

⚡ 35. Consider carefully your own use of smart technology.

How will knowing this help me?

Many parents, grandparents, caregivers, and child-development specialists share a deep concern about what smart technologies of various kinds (iPhones, iPads, Android tablets and phones, and so on) might be doing to the brains and abilities of today's infants, toddlers, and preschoolers.

Researchers are busy trying to design effective ways to study these effects. There is no doubt that brain changes will occur in children who are heavy users of technology from an early age. This is to be expected, knowing that the brain changes due to what we learn and what we devote time and attention to. We know this. However, we do not know whether the brain changes that will occur in this generation of young children will be something we value or something that we find harmful to them or to future generations.

The jury is still out on these important questions. We know, for example, that passive screen use, such as watching traditional television, is not recommended for infants and young toddlers under two years of age, as advised in a joint position statement from the National Association for the Education of Young Children and the Fred Rogers Center for Early Learning and Children's Media. Early research on iPads and interactive computer games is much less clear. Educator Warren Buckleitner, who studies children's use of technology, has noted that the characteristic of interaction itself is likely to bring positive results for many kinds of learning. Children learn that they have a sense of *agency*, or in other words *the power*, to make things happen on the screen. This notion that the child can direct the learning is a positive outcome.

Personally, I do not worry as much about what technology itself is doing to young children's brains by their own use of it. Rather, I wonder what unintended negative emotional messages are being sent by the nearly constant intrusion of the adults' technologies. Children learn very quickly that when parents or caregivers hear the ping of an incoming text or email, they are likely to withdraw from interacting with the children. Sometimes this happens for only a few seconds as the adult checks the nature of the message, but more often, the adult is preoccupied for the many minutes needed to read the message and respond. Parents and caregivers don't realize that this withdrawal or distraction can lead a child to feel that "Anybody is more important to you than I am!" Day after day, a child's meals, car rides, bedtime, and any time may revolve around the adult's smartphone. No matter how short the technology distraction, the child feels the disconnect. Attention to the child's needs suffers tremendously, and we just don't realize it at the time.

BRAIN NUGGET

Caregivers and parents need to beware of how their own use of technology sends harmful messages to young children by stealing attention from them in favor of the next incoming text.

Psychologist Catherine Steiner-Adair of Harvard Medical School has released a study about the impact of technology on the family unit. She studied more than 1,000 children, 500 parents, and 250 young adults, asking how they felt about technology in their lives. Overwhelmingly, the same five words were mentioned over and over by all age groups: *sad, mad, lonely, frustrated,* and *annoyed.* How alarming! She also reports that children have given up on their parent as the go-to person for help. Teachers and caregivers need to know that when they are in the presence of children, they need to continue to give them their full attention. A child needs to know that someone—a caregiver, if not a parent—is listening to and caring for him and not interrupting the moment to be virtually somewhere else on an electronic device.

The addiction that many of us have to our technologies is nearly universal, so do not feel guilty if you are hooked on texting or email. For all brains, it is compelling to know what is happening out there, and none of us wants to miss out. Our brains respond in predictable ways to the excitement of what might be waiting there for us. Because it is so compelling, we must work hard to voluntarily limit or exclude the use of our devices. Because it is hard to do, it really becomes a gift to children. It is a gift of attention. It is a gift of listening and of being present to interact with them.

So what should I try to do?

- Turn your devices off when you are caring for a child—all the way off.

- If you work at a child care center and find it really difficult to self-monitor and keep your device turned off, then it may be easier to turn it in at the preschool office for the duration of your workday. If someone needs to get in touch with you, she can call the center and leave a message. It is important that you be the person in a child's life who is present. It will mean a great deal to the overall emotional and cognitive development of that child.

- If you care for others' children in your home, limit your cell phone and computer use to incoming calls, texts, and emails only. When the children leave and you are done with your professional workday, then you can catch up on the day's news. You already know to have your television off, so add this to your list of important ways you can contribute to the best learning and loving environment possible for the children in your care, including your own!

- If you are a parent, please share this information with other adults in the home. Be mindful of the messages you purposefully and accidently send to your children. Each day, your child needs to know that he is the most important person in your life. If you work from home while caring for your child, be sure that you have designated someone else to be attentive to the needs of your child while you are focused on work. When you end your workday, purposefully put away your devices and be totally present and engaged with your child. You and your child will reap so many benefits in your relationships for a lifetime. Be the go-to person in your child's life.

Resources

Buckleitner, Warren. 2009. "What Should a Preschooler Know about Technology?" *Early Childhood Today*. http://www.scholastic.com/teachers/article/what-should -preschooler-know-about-technology

National Association for the Education of Young Children and the Fred Rogers Center for Early Learning and Children's Media at Saint Vincent College. 2012. *Technology and Interactive Media as Tools in Early Childhood Programs Serving Children from Birth through Age 8*. http://www.naeyc.org/files/naeyc/ PS_technology_WEB.pdf

Steiner-Adair, Catherine. 2013. *The Big Disconnect: Protecting Childhood and Family Relationships in the Digital Age.* New York: HarperCollins.

⚡ 36. Know that risk is not destiny.

How will knowing this help me?

Many of the factors that can serve to protect brain development and to combat poor outcomes for children are described in the strategies found in this book. It is interesting to study why some children, regardless of whatever combination of dire circumstances into which they were born, do grow up to develop sensitivity, normal or high intelligence, empathy for others, and positive self-regard. We all can think of countless examples and figures in history who have led extremely successful lives against all odds. When researchers study such fortunate mysteries, they find that it is not such a mystery after all.

Families, often with the help of close relatives, concerned neighbors, and assistance from social agencies, can and do develop protective factors that help to explain unexpected positive child outcomes. Support and encouragement can take different forms in different circumstances.

Well-documented research has found that poverty itself is an important contributor to delayed academic achievement, greater attention issues for children, increased discipline problems, and medical and dental concerns. However, various studies on the effects of protective factors show that caring adults can take steps to buffer the impact of poverty and adversity. The

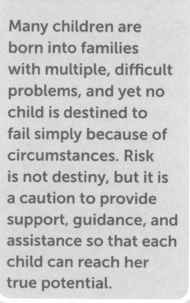

BRAIN NUGGET

Many children are born into families with multiple, difficult problems, and yet no child is destined to fail simply because of circumstances. Risk is not destiny, but it is a caution to provide support, guidance, and assistance so that each child can reach her true potential.

earlier in life a child receives consistent love and attention, the better the general outcome. However, it is also true that it is never too late to improve the life of a child. Because the brain has the quality of plasticity, improvements in daily life can, and do, produce positive brain changes.

So what should I try to do?

Parental *resilience*—the ability to bounce back from adversity—is important, and the reduction of stress adds to resilience. Therefore, strive to interact with parents of the children in your care in ways that will help them reduce stress. Offer suggestions of fun ways that they can engage with their children at home using simple, inexpensive materials. Positive parent-child interactions can help relieve household stress.

- Provide handouts or have conversations with parents about child development. Sharing age-appropriate expectations can be especially helpful.

- Create gatherings where parents of the children you care for can come together for fun and mutual support. Social connectedness helps to prevent social isolation often experienced by families in need.

- Determine whether local social-services agencies offer parenting classes or other helpful sessions; if so, consider distributing registration information.

- Model the kind of respect that children need from the adults in their lives. Demonstrate how to show affection for and respect the dignity of each child.

- While children are in your care, make sure to meet their basic needs for safety, nutrition, and health. Hungry, sick, or frightened children cannot learn effectively. Determine the correct process at your center, or in your community, for referrals to help children have their essential needs attended to.

Resources

Child Welfare Information Gateway. 2014. *Protective Factors Approaches in Child Welfare.* Child Welfare Information Gateway. https://childwelfare.gov/pubPDFs /protective_factors.pdf

Masten, Ann S., and Norman Garmezy. 1985. "Risk, Vulnerability, and Protective Factors in Developmental Psychopathology." In *Advances in Clinical Child Psychology,* vol. 8, edited by Benjamin B. Lahey and Alan E. Kazdin, 1–52. New York: Plenum Press.

⚡ 37. Learn about and practice mindfulness.

How will knowing this help me?

Mindfulness is currently a hot topic in the news. In our modern society, we are becoming aware that too many things are competing for our attention and we sometimes need help to focus better and stay the course for becoming a better parent or caregiver for young children. We live in an era of ultraconnectivity (smartphones, iPads, Android tablets), yet many individuals are feeling desperately alone. We find ourselves wondering how we can slow it all down because we just can't keep up! A pill? A drink? A massage? Yoga? Meditation? A person may think, "Maybe mindfulness is something I can do. What is it?"

Mindfulness is the moment-by-moment awareness of our thoughts, emotions, and environment, characterized mainly by acceptance and by giving attention to thoughts and feelings without judging whether they are right or wrong. You can become more mindful by practicing yoga, meditation, or reflection. The goal is to slow down the constant input you are bombarded with so that you can be calmer and more present with the people in your life. Mindfulness alerts us to the notion that we can learn to focus better and feel better. Mindfulness has emerged as a way to combat all that comes too fast and, often, way too soon.

For caregivers and parents, mindfulness involves interacting with children on

BRAIN NUGGET

Learning how to become more mindful in your daily interactions with children can result in their improved social-emotional and intellectual growth.

purpose in ways that help, rather than simply following your instincts. In other words, mindfulness requires being conscious of your actions and words to stay true to your goals for children's healthy development.

Be intentional in your actions with and for children. Mindfulness involves learning to focus on the present and recruits strategies that have a long history, such as meditation, chanting, and yoga. These practices have been adapted to our modern, fast-paced world that is overloaded with too much stuff and too much stress. But it is hard to focus our attention on the present. Amishi Jha, one of the leading scientists in attention research, says the practice is like shining a flashlight on what you want to stay focused on. Try keeping that light on the present instead of wandering off into the future or the past.

Most people have a difficult time staying in the moment. We worry constantly about what could happen if…. Or we try to stay ahead of things by planning the next day, next vacation, next year, and so on. We blast through the moment to get to the weekend. We do all these things instead of living right now.

Neuroscientific evidence now shows that engaging in mindfulness practices can positively affect the brain and the body in restorative ways. This practice can potentially reduce stress, lower blood pressure, treat depression, reduce hypertension, and increase energy and alertness. If you are interested in learning more about the benefits of mindfulness, look at the work of Jon Kabat-Zinn, founding executive director of the Center for Mindfulness in Medicine, Health Care, and Society at the University of Massachusetts Medical School.

So what should I try to do?

Start by simply noticing.

- Notice where you are.
- Notice how you feel.
- Notice the people in your life.
- Notice the changes that are happening around you.
- Notice the changes in your own being.

Begin by noticing your environment or how relaxed or tense you are at a given moment. For example, note where you are holding your shoulders. If you are holding tension there, use this information to make a shift and let your shoulders relax and fall. One of the hardest things to notice may be the small but evident changes in your own well-being. Taking care of children is a hard job. It is demanding. It takes time and energy as well as education to provide quality care. As a caregiver, you need to care for yourself first.

Mindfulness training is one way you can do some rewiring to strengthen your own pathways and ability to do the following:

- Focus

- Calm yourself

- Stay optimistic

- Feel connected to something larger than your circumstances

You already know some strategies that work. For a child, or someone acting like a child, taking a breath can help. For an adolescent, you might suggest just chilling out for a bit. For caregivers, you can remind yourself to take five, count to ten, sleep on it, or stop and smell the roses.

Here are several other strategies you can try:

- Take steps to turn off your devices (emails, texts, phone calls) whenever you can. This action limits the incoming noise that bombards each of us.

- Limit your multitasking. Research from the American Psychological Association shows us that it doesn't really work. The psychological perception of being able to do two things at once is an illusion. What you are really doing is task switching. When you do rapid task switching, you lose accuracy. That comes with a cost in your brain as well. You pay by having less accuracy and increased stress on the attention system, which selects information, and on the working memory, which maintains information to keep it available for use.

If you are going to multitask, try to choose activities that will not require serious attention to detail or that will recruit different brain regions, such as visual and auditory rather than auditory and auditory.

Find strategies and exercises that work for you. Borrow some aspects of time-honored teachings, and make efforts to stay in the moment:

- Focus on your breath—This is the most common and the most portable approach.

- Make a full-body scan—Relax, breathe slowly, take note of each part of your body separately, and consciously think of letting go of any tension that might be held there.

- Do yoga poses—These can be done alone or in a class setting.

- Chant or count—Many religions have various ways to chant or count that have been used for centuries (for example, using rosary beads in the Catholic religion).

- Practice mindful walking, eating, and watching—Consciously slow down the simple, automatic things you do each day in order to experience each more fully.

- Engage in mental reflection—Bring experiences you have had back into focus. Think about the details of those experiences and what you remember and why.

- Meditate—If you are interested in exploring meditation, visit Martin Boroson's site, One-Moment Meditation, and view the video "How to Meditate in a Moment."

Resources

American Psychological Association. 2006. "Multitasking: Switching Costs." *Research in Action*. http://www.apa.org/research/action/multitask.aspx

Boroson, Martin. 2011. "How to Meditate in a Moment." *One-Moment Meditation*. http://www.onemomentmeditation.com

Davidson, Richard J., et al. 2012. "Contemplative Practices and Mental Training: Prospects for American Education." *Child Development Perspectives* 6(2): 146–153.

Kabat-Zinn, Jon. 2005. *Wherever You Go, There You Are.* New York: Hachette.

Morrison, Alexandra, et al. 2014. "Taming a Wandering Attention: Short-Form Mindfulness Training in Student Cohorts." *Frontiers in Human Neuroscience* 7(897): 1–2. http://journal.frontiersin.org/article/10.3389/fnhum.2013.00897/full

PART 6
Communication Messages

⚡ 38. Realize the power of a face.

How will knowing this help me?

Babies' visual systems are designed to help them clearly see their primary caregivers, who are key to their survival. Usually the caregiver's face shows signs of love while caring for the child, whether the activity is feeding, cuddling, or rocking.

For the child, the facial expression most associated with getting needs met becomes a smiling, cooing, loving configuration of the caregiver's eyes and mouth. Babies and young children quickly become experts in learning that variations from what they expect—the gentle, loving facial expression—may carry different meanings. Changes in *affect*—which is the general feeling, tone, and emotion expressed by a person—become signals to the child of possible changes in responsive care.

For example, a baby tends to notice the flat affect of a depressed caregiver—lack of facial expression, no smile, and fixed eyes—and then shows immediate distress by becoming agitated and fussy and by averting her own eye gaze. Likewise, the

> **BRAIN NUGGET**
>
> The brain shows a preference for upright faces. Being able to understand the meaning or intention of facial expressions is one key to survival.

glare of an angry eye or a firmly set mouth signals concern not only because it is a change from the expected joyful face but also because it may link to stiff jerky movements, abrupt ending to a feeding, and harsh tones in speaking. Children remember the facial configuration linked to stern treatment.

So what should I try to do?

- Every once in a while, someone may walk by you and say, "Smile!" You probably don't even know you have a serious look on your face. But babies are constantly making primal interpretations of caregivers' faces, wondering if the person near them will be kind to them or not. Be sure that you show genuine love and caring not only by your actions but also by your facial expressions.

- If you are feeling down, try to perk up your behavior and your facial expressions before interacting with children. It can help you as well. Several research studies have shown that smiling not only makes you look happier but also can make you feel good.

- If you are severely depressed, get help for yourself. Until you feel better, ask coworkers to help with the direct care of children.

- If you are angry, get immediate coverage for the children in your care, and remove yourself from caregiving. Return only when you can genuinely be emotionally positive and available to care for children.

Resources

Goleman, Daniel. 1989. "A Feel-Good Theory: A Smile Affects Mood." *New York Times*, July 18, http://www.nytimes.com/1989/07/18/science/a-feel-good-theory-a-smile-affects-mood.html?sec=&spon=&pagewanted=all

McClure, Max. 2012. "Infants Process Faces Long Before They Recognize Other Objects, Stanford Vision Researchers Find." *Stanford Report.* http://news.stanford.edu/news/2012/december/infants-process-faces-121112.html

Zajonc, Robert B. 1985. "Emotion and Facial Efference: A Theory Reclaimed." *Science* 228(4695): 15–21.

⚡ 39. Talk, talk, talk!

How will knowing this help me?

Some now-famous research studies from Betty Hart and Todd Risley have shown that there are vast differences in the amount of talk directed at young children in households across the United States. The sheer number of words spoken to a child was recorded, along with whether the tone of the utterance was positive or negative. When the researchers plotted the results of their findings, they saw that the number of words correlated roughly with the economic status of the family, with families in lower socioeconomic homes speaking 616 words, in working-class homes speaking 1,251 words, and in professional homes using more than 2,153 words. Researchers then looked at how the number of words compared with the later testable IQ of the children, and they found a direct linear relationship.

One of the main messages remains hidden in the economics, however. If a parent from a very low-income home decides to talk, talk, talk while narrating a child's day and engages the child with lots of descriptive, interesting words and positive conversation, the outcome might be a higher IQ for the child, based again on the number of words. This is great news!

So what should I try to do?

- As you work with young children, be mindful of what this research really means. Talk to and engage children in language-rich environments on purpose. When you provide lots of books and songs and stories that use interesting words that expand a child's world, that child's mind expands as well. The power of words, although detectable by age three, does not stop. Increases in vocabulary are critical to reading comprehension and to concept development throughout a child's schooling and beyond.

BRAIN NUGGET

The sheer number of words spoken to a child from birth to age three has a direct impact on his later testable IQ. Research shows that talking and being read to often can actually increase a child's IQ.

- The message to caregivers and teachers at any level is to engage children in language-rich environments for many purposes. Finding new games and fun strategies to motivate children to learn and use new vocabulary words is a responsibility we all share.

- If you provide care for someone else's children, share this message with the family, so the child can benefit in multiple ways from this research-supported strategy.

Resources

Hart, Betty, and Todd R. Risley. 2003. "The Early Catastrophe: The 30 Million Word Gap by Age 3." *American Educator* 4–9. Accessed March 26, 2015. http://www.aft.org/ae/spring2003/hart_risley

Hart, Betty, and Todd R. Risley. 1995. *Meaningful Differences in the Everyday Experience of Young American Children.* Baltimore: Paul H. Brookes Publishing Co.

⚡ 40. Use the voice that comes naturally when you talk to a baby.

How will knowing this help me?

In many cultures throughout the world, parents use a high-pitched, exaggerated speech pattern when talking to their babies. That happens because caring adults notice that the baby looks at and seems to be paying attention to them when they do that! It seems to be a feedback loop, in that the more the baby pays attention to your exaggerated talk, the more you tend do it. You say, "Oooooh, loook at this sweeeet little faaace." The baby alerts to our voice as if to say, "Tell me more!" You speak slowly and elongate the vowels so that the baby follows along better. You most likely use this way of speaking when you are face-to-face and very close so that the baby can also watch your mouth.

It is magical how well this way of speaking matches the processing speed of the baby's brain as it wires up to detect speech sounds! And most amazing of all is that no one instructed you to do this! You do it because you care about the baby and want to connect. Quite naturally, as the baby develops and gets older, we begin to speed up our pace and return to normal speaking tones to keep up with the child's interest level.

Parentese is not the same as *baby talk*, which may use nonsense words or syllables, such as *da-da* and *na-na-na-na*. Those types of vocalizations are appropriate when the baby starts to babble and test what sounds she can produce. When the baby makes a sound, at first by accident and then on

BRAIN NUGGET

Parentese is a natural and universal way of talking to a baby that slows down and exaggerates the vowel sounds in words while using a high-pitched speaking voice. It is interesting that this way of speaking matches perfectly with the speed and frequency that an infant's brain can clearly hear and most easily process! Use real words, but exaggerate the sounds.

purpose, it is important to imitate that sound and vocalize it back. These interactions form the start of language communication. The baby makes a sound, and you respond, and then she responds, and so on. At a very early age, babies begin to anticipate that when they make a sound, you will repeat it. Language has begun!

So what should I try to do?

Now that you know the significance of these forms of early communication, you can be confident that your natural powers of attending to and caring for young children are real strengths. Try some of the following strategies regularly:

- Use parentese and have fun noticing how a young baby's attention shifts toward you when you are speaking.

- Try to think about and notice when your pace begins to change.

- Babble back to the infant who is enjoying finding her voice. Try to extend the back-and-forth pattern and encourage the baby to keep the volley going.

- Try to initiate some new sounds while you are up close and personal to see if the baby will try to match and imitate your sounds.

Have fun playing with these early language communications!

⚡ 41. Articulate speech sounds accurately because a child's ability to hear these sounds can affect the child's success in learning to talk.

How will knowing this help me?

The auditory processing centers of the brain have nerve cells that are poised to respond to specific frequencies of sound heard in the environment. Specific neurons are tuned to react when that certain sound occurs. Our ability to hear language then depends on our brain's ability to receive and recognize the individual tones, patterns, and rhythms of sound. Hearing individual speech sounds accurately is important as the child tries to talk and produce those same sounds.

Most babies are born with normal hearing. However, young children who have frequent ear infections may not be able to accurately hear those individual differences in speech sounds during a flare-up of inflammation associated with infection. Observant caregivers might begin to notice that a young child who was previously making appropriate babbling sounds and starting to try to say words may suddenly stop or significantly slow down his speech attempts. It is a good idea to monitor this possibility when a parent or caregiver notices that the child is sick, has a severe cold, is pulling at the ear, or has recently been diagnosed with an ear infection.

BRAIN NUGGET

Children who can hear the differences in sounds—distinguishing one sound from another—will later have an easier time learning to talk.

So what should I try to do?

- Enunciate and pronounce your speech sounds clearly. Make sure the young child you are speaking to can see your mouth and lips. When you are sure that he can see you clearly, you may want to also let him see your teeth and tongue for certain sounds. Babies and young toddlers need to see how to produce speech.

- Communicate with all caregivers if a child is sick or shows signs of an ear infection. Notice delays or changes in the attempt to talk. Caregivers should carefully observe children's speaking progress, document any concerns, and strive for open communication about any issues.

- Some young early talkers may slow their production of sounds even when they are not sick. Children show great variability in the rate and path of development as they learn to talk. You will notice individual variations appearing not only among children but also from the same child at different times. Don't let the differences alarm you too soon, but stay alert and have parents consult a doctor if concerns remain.

⚡ 42. Try using sign language with preverbal children.

How will knowing this help me?

As you recall, the brain is an energy-conserving organ. Because the visual system develops so early and is the first of the cognitive systems to be hard-wired and ready for use, it is easy for the young brain to process visual input. Visual processing therefore uses less energy than other systems at an early age. Signing takes advantage of this early development.

Gestures have always been an important way that humans communicate. Nonverbal communication can even override verbal communication when there is confusion about the meaning of an interaction.

Sign language, which uses a combination of hand, finger, and arm movements, can aid communication with people who are hearing impaired or deaf. It can also help bridge the gap of communication with infants and toddlers before they can easily verbalize their thoughts. With young children, you can begin using a few survival signs regularly to help the child learn the meaning of them.

Recurring questions about the use of sign language with very young children include the following:

- **Will a child's verbal language be slowed down by the use of sign language?**

  No. There is no evidence that using sign language slows down typically developing verbal skills. In fact, sign language may actually jump-start

BRAIN NUGGET

The use of sign language can alleviate some of the distress that young toddlers feel when they cannot yet verbally communicate their wants and needs before their expressive language skills can catch up.

verbal development as the child quickly learns that she can play an active role in communication. Typically, a child will easily transition from the use of signs to a more universal way of using words for expressing wants and needs as well as more elaborate questions and comments on the world.

- **If you use sign language with a young child, will it increase her IQ?**

  Findings from researchers vary. Some studies show early IQ gains from using sign language that typically fade as children become verbal. Other studies have shown more lasting evidence of cognitive gains. A number of factors may play a role, including the tendency to communicate more as the caregiver and child experience less frustration and anxiety during interactions.

- **What are the reasons an adult might want to use sign language with young children?**

  Signing can help the adult feel tuned in to the child. Once the baby or toddler has at least ten signs, the adult spends less energy trying to figure out what the child wants and can spend more time interacting with and enjoying that child. Never underestimate the value of being more relaxed and enjoying yourself and your job!

For the young child, having these tools can lessen the frustration of wanting to communicate with a caregiver. In turn, smoother interactions can facilitate bonding by helping the caregiver and the child feel less anxious and more relaxed. When a child is less anxious, there is more cognitive energy available in her brain for learning!

So what should I try to do?

You might want to start by teaching several survival signs to babies or young toddlers:

- *eat*
- *more*
- *done*
- *sleep*
- *milk*
- *change* (as in change diaper)

You can look online for sites that will diagram or demonstrate typical signs for these words.

You can start to use these signs when the child is about four or five months old, but do not expect the baby to complete the circle of communication by making the sign until seven to nine months of age. Before then, the infant is not likely to have the physical coordination to control motor movements needed to imitate the gestures.

If the baby likes and will use these basic signs, you might want to elaborate and add some of the following:

- *help*
- *water* (or drink)
- *hot*
- *cold*

Then you can add any of the kinds of activities children may come to love and be able to anticipate, such as some in the list that follows. If you start to use these signs early as you begin such interactions, a child will begin to anticipate what is coming next. This ability to predict what is coming is an important cognitive skill and one that a brain is biased to do naturally. If you can predict what will happen next, you are better prepared and can survive better.

- *play*
- *bath*
- *book*
- *ball*
- *ride in the car*
- *go to daycare* (grandma, neighbor, center)

Signs you might add for older children include the following:

- *share*
- *please*
- *thank you*

Be consistent. Make eye contact to be sure that the child can see your gestures. Say the word as you make the sign. This will help the child learn the word and associate the concept with the gesture.

Show excitement that the two of you are communicating!

Resources

Acredolo, Linda, and Susan Goodwyn. 2002. *Baby Signs: How to Talk with Your Baby Before Your Baby Can Talk.* Rev. ed. New York: McGraw-Hill.

Daniels, Marilyn. 1994. "The Effect of Sign Language on Hearing Children's Language Development." *Communication Education* 43(4): 291–298.

Goodwyn, Susan W., Linda P. Acredolo, and Catherine A. Brown. 2000. "Impact of Symbolic Gesturing on Early Language Development." *Journal of Nonverbal Behavior* 24(2): 81–103.

⚡ 43. Learn that actually playing a musical instrument is better than just listening for children's brain development.

How will knowing this help me?

Over the past few decades, many promoters have claimed that if babies just listen to recordings of classical music, then their math and science test scores increase later in life. To date, I know of no study that has shown this to be an effective approach. What does appear to change brain structure is actually learning to play and practice playing a musical instrument such as the violin or the piano at a young age.

BRAIN NUGGET

Classical music is known to relax adults and children when they listen to it, but it probably doesn't change brain structure.

So how did this notion get started? Researchers did find that the relaxation and focus effect of listening to classical music immediately prior to taking a college-entrance test such as the SAT College Admission Exam did tend to increase students' scores on the test. Analysts then extrapolated that if such a practice of just listening could help high school students on a high-stakes test, it must make amazing differences for an infant's brain as it is developing. This part of the story is not supported by evidence.

There is, however, interesting research conducted by Ellen Winner at Boston College and Gottfried Schlaug at Harvard in a long-term study that used brain imaging to look at brain changes in children that could be attributed to playing a musical instrument. They found growth in children's brain regions associated with cognitive skills related to spatial, motor, and verbal development.

The brain changes through use. When a person activates particular brain regions for a task, those areas tend to respond and grow. So it makes sense that these changes would be found. Again, there are no such changes found from simply hearing classical music.

So what does listening to this type of music do? For adults, you will likely find that listening to classical music seems to relax you and perhaps the infants in your care as well. Naturally, when the people in a room are more relaxed, the overall environment tends to be more relaxed as well.

So what should I try to do?

- Try listening to Mozart to see if you experience any relaxation response. Some researchers have suggested that the particular number of beats per minute in many Mozart compositions mirrors the firing patterns of a brain when it is relaxed. In addition to Mozart's music, recognize that many other classical music selections may have the same effect.

- Play classical music, along with many other types of music, for the children in your care. Engage young children in playing beginning instruments. *Musical involvement*, which encompasses listening to music, singing songs, and playing musical instruments, is important to overall intellectual development.

- Not only music involvement, but also frequent talking, reading, and listening to rhymes are important to later intellectual development.

⚡ 44. Use bold colors with young infants, but don't get carried away for long.

How will knowing this help me?

Infants tend to notice objects in bold colors such as black, white, red, and yellow, especially when used in combination. When these colors are combined in bold patterns, they can capture and keep an infant's attention because of what is happening in the brain. The brain's visual centers are busy wiring up to develop what is called *figure-ground discrimination*, which is the ability to distinguish an object from its background. High contrast, such as a black square against a white background, provides an opportunity to first see the edges of something. Being able to see the edges is important in learning where something begins and ends.

By about four months, a baby's visual system is wired to see objects and people as well as a wide range of colors and shapes. The infant also has developed enough depth perception to be able to reach for and grab the toy of her choice. By six months, the visual system of the baby is sophisticated enough that she can clearly see people and things in her everyday environment.

So what should I try to do?

- If you are caring for an infant, remember that in the first few months of life, an infant's primary focus is on colorful objects 8 to 10 inches from her face or the distance to a parent's or caregiver's face when she is nursing or drinking from a bottle. Recall also that infants prefer human faces to other stimuli, regardless of how cute or colorful the object might be.

- If you are caring for an older baby, keep in mind that babies have good color vision by four to five months of age. Eye-hand coordination begins to develop as the babies track moving objects with their eyes and begin to reach for them. During months five to eight, control of eye movements and eye-body coordination skills continue to improve. By the sixth month, the eyes are capable of working together to form a three-dimensional view of the world and begin to see in depth.

- Many babies begin to crawl by about eight months old, which helps the continued development of eye-hand and eye-body coordination. Early walkers, who might have had minimal crawling, may not at first learn to use their eyes together as well as babies who crawl a lot.

> **BRAIN NUGGET**
>
> During infancy, stimulation of a baby's visual perception is enhanced by exposure to bold colors and patterns, and moving objects. Rapidly, however, the brain's visual centers wire up to see all colors and more complex patterns.

⚡ 45. Watch what is done—to know what to do.

How will knowing this help me?

Anyone who has cared for young children knows that they learn by imitating what they see other people do. It turns out that there is a scientific reason.

In the 1980s, some Italian neuroscientists made an accidental discovery while working in their lab with monkeys. These monkeys were surgically hooked up to machines that read their brain activations, showing which regions were working as they made various movements. During a lunch break, one of the monkeys saw a scientist make a series of arm movements while bringing an ice cream cone to his lips. Even though the monkey did not move at all, the scientist noticed activation in the same parts of the monkey's brain as those that would have been working if he were making the gestures of eating an ice cream cone. This discovery led to an entire area of study to determine what these neurons that reacted this way were responsible for. The scientists called these specialized neurons *mirror neurons* and jokingly said this new discovery explains the old saying, "Monkey see, monkey do."

A series of studies have now shown that many behaviors that a person sees are experienced in the brain in the identical regions that would activate if the person were actually doing the behavior himself. It seems that the brain is practicing having the experience without actually doing it. This finding helps to explain why someone watching football on TV will wince and have a sense of physical pain when seeing a player injured during a powerful football tackle. It helps explain how someone can learn by just watching a teacher, a parent, or another child do an activity. We imitate what we see. Our mirror neurons have shortened our learning curve.

The same is true for emotions. We cry in sad movies and feel frightened when we see someone hit another person. None of these things are happening to us, but we feel them nevertheless.

So what should I try to do?

- Use this knowledge to your advantage. Model what you want another person to do. Demonstrate. Act in ways that will entice someone to learn. Be clear. Show exactly what is needed for another person to do what you are doing.

- Know that positive behaviors, such as feeding a baby doll, and negative behaviors, such as yelling when a situation does not go your way, will be learned through these imitation brain circuits.

- The emotional climate you create will be learned by the children in your care. If you say one thing yet do another, then children are likely to learn what you do. Reflect on how children will mirror the responses of other children. If one starts to cry, others may follow. If one starts to laugh, others may start to giggle themselves. Be mindful of what emotions are present, and build on this mirroring effect to achieve harmony in your classroom or home.

- Know that the emotions a young child sees, and therefore can feel, can be internalized without your knowledge. Therefore, maintain courteous, respectful behaviors among the adults in your environment. Children are learning about emotional conflict and support long before they can verbalize it.

Resources

Rizzollati, Giacomo, and Laila Craighero. 2004. "The Mirror-Neuron System." *Annual Review of Neuroscience* 27: 169–192.

Winerman, Lea. 2005. "The Mind's Mirror." *Monitor on Psychology* 36(9): 48. http://www.apa.org/monitor/oct05/mirror.aspx

BRAIN NUGGET

In recent decades, scientists have discovered new kinds of neurons called *mirror neurons*. These neurons have a unique characteristic in that they fire, or activate, both when a person simply observes someone else carrying out an action and when the person actually carries out an action himself. This discovery that there are brain regions that activate during both observed and performed actions is the beginning of understanding how and why imitation is one of the main ways that humans learn from each other. These findings extend beyond just observing and performing physical actions and apply to expressing and experiencing emotions as well.

⚡ 46. Learn why so many children seem to love puppets.

How will knowing this help me?

Puppets are loved by children for different reasons at different stages of development.

Note that the act of playing with the puppet causes the child to want to keep interacting and having fun. Having fun results in repetition, and the repetition of playing actually causes the important brain changes of learning.

Initially, puppets that have high contrast and bright colors capture a baby's attention. Motion and high-contrast colors engage an infant's rapidly developing visual regions in the brain.

You can captivate a child by what you choose to make the puppet say. Young children learning how to talk will pay especially close attention to the puppet's mouth area as you move it in rhythm with your words. Interest in words and language engages the auditory regions in the brain as well as the motor regions that control mouth movements used to create speech.

Older toddlers, as well as preschoolers, will take control of the puppet and use it to express themselves. They make the puppet speak. They share their feelings through what the puppet says. The important job of learning to manage her emotions is central to the common themes in a young child's imaginary play. Fear, anger, frustration, joy, and exuberance are prime-time puppet fare! Learning impulse control and emotional regulation engage the frontal and central structures of the developing brain.

So what should I try to do?

- With infants, you can play with brightly colored puppets that have a discernible mouth area that is visible. Talk using slow, high-pitched, clearly enunciated words to keep the infant engaged. Move the puppet to reengage and hold an infant's attention while she tries to track the moving and dancing puppet.

- With young toddlers, colorful puppets can be an excellent language starter as you engage children in conversations with the puppets. Silly, fun physical contact—such as touching, gentle tickles, and kisses—from the puppet to the child tend to delight her. As the toddler begins to show interest, encourage her to touch and hold the puppet herself.

BRAIN NUGGET

Puppets have enduring appeal. While infants are developing their visual systems, older babies and toddlers are developing their language centers, and toddlers and preschoolers are developing emotional regulation, their brains are tuned to learn important skills from a caregiver's knowledgeable use of puppets.

- Older toddlers and preschoolers may confide in puppets and feel emotional connections to them. Preschoolers use puppets to help act out new ideas or tasks they are learning and new emotions they want to express. Taking control of the puppet encourages a sense of agency, or the ability to feel in control, that is important at this stage.

⚡ 47. Repeat the same book; it's OK.

How will knowing this help me?

The next time young children ask you to read *Goodnight Moon* yet again, indulge them. Reading a book again and again may seem tedious to you, but it is important for the great learning that is going on in a child's brain! Repetition of the connections from one neuron to another is how learning and memory are strengthened. Each time a repetition occurs, a fatty, protective covering called myelin deposits on parts of the neuron. Myelin works like an insulator, allowing the electrical charge within the neural network to flow more easily and more rapidly. As with an electrical cord in your house, the insulation keeps the electrical charge from leaking out of the neuron and prevents interruptions in the flow of the charge.

BRAIN NUGGET

Many children love to have you read the same book over and over. The human brain learns best through repetition. So go ahead. Know that each reading is a chance to strengthen learning.

When you repeat or rehearse something that you have already learned, the connections in your brain get stronger, and eventually the skill or knowledge you have will become almost automatic. Once that occurs, your brain uses very little conscious energy to accomplish that learned task. Young children, who are busy learning everything for the first time, need practice to make life easier. Many of the things that are initially a struggle will later go on automatic pilot.

When you reread a book to children, they already know what happens. Knowing feels good and allows them to relax because they already understand what will happen in the familiar story. In a world where so much is still unknown and unfamiliar, the certainty that is achieved through repetition is wonderful. Focusing on the familiar frees up the child's brain energy to extend and elaborate on the knowledge he already has.

So what should I try to do?

- Rereading a familiar story provides the perfect opportunity to expand on information the children already know. You can engage in a dialogue about why they think some particular event happened. You can point out details they may not have noticed before. Extend, elaborate, and build new vocabulary to describe ideas found in the book.

- Some toddlers and many preschoolers will eventually be able to recite, almost verbatim, each page of the story. They love to think they are reading the pages. A few might be! Most will actually have memorized the familiar words that are cued by the pictures on the page. This is wonderful exercise for a child's memory skills.

- A multiage setting provides a great opportunity for an older child to read favorite stories to a younger child.

- Repeated readings also encourage greater book knowledge—orienting the print in an upright fashion, turning pages, and so on.

⚡ 48. Be sure to point to objects when teaching new words.

How will knowing this help me?

Young children learn to speak and remember the names of objects much more rapidly when you point and look at the object while giving the name. Children will then look in the direction of your finger and your gaze to focus on the object you are naming. Research has shown that this quality, called *joint attention,* is critical for language learning.

Pointing while labeling seems to come naturally to most people who are trying to teach a young child the names of things. The importance of *shared gaze,* both the child and the adult looking at the same thing at the same time, may be a new idea to many caregivers but probably occurs easily as well.

Research has found that some children with autism have difficulty following a pointing finger. Researchers are conducting studies to determine how this may be related to language delays in many autistic children.

So what should I try to do?

- As you read a book with a child and teach the names of new objects, say the name and point to the object at the same time, on purpose instead of by accident.

- Check to be sure that your eyes and the child's eyes are both looking at the same thing. What you are looking for is to see that a shared gaze is actually occurring.

- Once a child's verbal skills have developed enough to repeat the name of the object after you have said it, ask, "Can you say the word?" Then prompt, "Say it again."

BRAIN NUGGET

As you read to a child, point to the pictures in the book. Does the child look at what you are pointing to? Pointing is a developmental milestone and is a uniquely human capability.

Resources

Baron-Cohen, Simon. 1989. "Perceptual Role Taking and Protodeclarative Pointing in Autism." *British Journal of Developmental Psychology* 7(2): 113–127.

Brooks, Rechele, and Andrew N. Meltzoff. 2005. "The development of gaze following and its relation to language." *Developmental Science* 8(6): 535–543.

Child Talk. 2011. "Red Flags for Autism in Toddlers." *Child Talk*. http://www.talkingkids.org/2011/04/red-flags-for-autism-in-toddlers.html

Clements, Caitlin, and Katarzyna Chawarska. 2010. "Beyond Pointing: Development of the 'Showing' Gesture in Children with Autism Spectrum Disorder." *The Yale Review of Undergraduate Research in Psychology:* 46–63.

⚡ 49. Read books and sing songs that have rhyme, rhythm, and repetition.

How will knowing this help me?

When scientists have studied some common reading difficulties, such as dyslexia, it turns out that many reading issues are not visual, as many people have guessed in the past, but are actually auditory-processing problems. For example, if a child cannot hear the differences between *p-a-t, c-a-t, s-a-t,* and *r-a-t,* he cannot effectively learn to read the differences. Recently, reading experts have invented computer-based programs that put children through listening exercises to build up their ability to hear distinct differences in *phonemes,* the small units of sound. Once children can hear the differences, they typically have success in learning to read. However, such programs are remedial and are often very expensive.

Books that have rhymes structured throughout can provide helpful exposure in a natural setting. Emphasizing rhyming is easy and fun and can prevent the development of future reading problems in learners. In addition to rhymes, most phrases and songs that children love tend to have lots of rhythm because they have a steady beat. The rhymes and rhythms follow a typical pattern that gets repeated over and over again.

Rhyme, rhythm, and repetition form a perfect trio and have become the new three *R*'s for helping prepare future learners. Research has shown that young children who can keep a steady beat in a song or chant have an easier time learning how to read.

So what should I try to do?

- For children of all ages, read stories that have lots of rhyming. For example, the silliness of the rhymes in Dr. Seuss books often makes children pay attention and laugh, but the structure of the rhyming is the real value of such books.

- Listening to and singing songs is also important and can be lots of fun. The repetition and rhythm of children's favorites make them easy to remember and provide the enjoyment needed to keep rehearsing them.

- Because learning how to keep a steady beat to music is so important, clapping sequences with chants or dancing to the pace of a song not only are fun, but also provide the practice needed to develop new learning skills. Learning to play with simple rhythmic instruments such as the bells, triangle, or drums is also a way to practice keeping the beat.

BRAIN NUGGET

Learning to read effectively and efficiently is dependent on a child's ability to hear the small differences in speech sounds, called *phonemic awareness*. Therefore, practice with rhyming is critical to the later development of reading.

Resources

Woodruff Carr, Kali, et al. 2014. "Beat Synchronization Predicts Neural Speech Encoding and Reading Readiness in Preschoolers." *Proceedings of the National Academy of Sciences, USA* 111(40): 14559–14564.

⚡ 50. Read books aloud to build a child's conceptual development.

How will knowing this help me?

The general public sometimes gets confused as to why reading books with very young children is important. Caregivers wonder if they are supposed to be trying to teach a baby or toddler how to read! Intuitively, adults know that this is not a fun or productive activity. Recently, to add to the confusion, a company was advertising products to help babies learn to read. First of all, babies don't need to know how to read! These ideas are misguided.

So why do caregivers read to babies and toddlers? Reading exposes young children to lots and lots of new words, but we also use new words as we describe what we see in the pictures or discuss what we think about the stories. The real beauty of reading books with young children emerges during discussions about the story or the illustrations. This is where the personal moments of sharing your own memories happen. This is where emotions are exchanged. This is where the interactions around words, stories, and books intersect with a shared love of being together.

A love of learning most often starts with a love of the experiences that get associated with learning.

> **BRAIN NUGGET**
>
> Reading to young children introduces new vocabulary and reinforces familiar concepts. Sharing a book with a child gives the child a lot to think and talk about!

So what should I try to do?

- Read daily to each child you are caring for. Sometimes to accomplish this, you will need to have short sessions. Then you can set a goal to increase the frequency and duration of these short reading sessions.

- Share your thoughts and feelings about what you are reading. Some children's books have few words but are rich with concepts. These concepts are often introduced through pictures and illustrations. Talk, talk, talk.

- It is also important to ask questions. Ask a child to point to what you are talking about. When a young child has developed some expressive language, ask her to tell you what is happening or what might happen next. Pointing while labeling the names of objects, people, and things is a critical aspect for the child to be able to learn new vocabulary words.

⚡ 51. Try proactive approaches in early reading strategies.

How will knowing this help me?

Researchers who study brain images know that the brain-activation patterns of adults and older children with dyslexia differ from the brain-activation patterns of effective readers.

Specific remedial efforts to change the brain's wiring in the differing regions to support reading have been successful, as Sally Shaywitz notes in her book *Overcoming Dyslexia*. Through intense and often costly methods that focus on phonemic awareness, brain patterns can change, brain regions that were not very active can become active, and a child receiving such intense intervention can become a successful reader. One of the main strategies for fine-tuning the brain's ability to detect differences in sounds is to practice exercises involving rhyming.

BRAIN NUGGET

Because the brain wires naturally to be able to hear differences in speech sounds, be proactive and provide lots of practice with rhyming words and sounds. You may be able to avoid future reading problems such as dyslexia.

So what should I try to do?

- During infancy, play with speech sounds. Repeat the babbling sounds that a baby makes back to him. Be playful and extend and initiate beginning attempts to imitate these sounds.

- Read simple books to infants, and tell stories to expose them to lots of words, including rhyming words.

- Focus on reading rhyming books with toddlers. Find some favorites, and read these often. Emphasize the rhymes and the repetition of phrases. Luckily, many of these also have the rhythm of a steady beat.

- Play with speech sounds often with toddlers. If the child says *hot*, repeat *hot* and start to find other words that rhyme, such as *dot*, *got*, *lot*, *shot*, and *spot*. Children will enjoy this word play and will begin to try random sounds to see if they make sense. You will find that you can do this with children endlessly. They love it and it doesn't cost a penny; you don't need special equipment or flashcards!

- For preschoolers, play games with words to see if they can spy words that rhyme as you read together. This gives them a fun way to practice visual searching as well.

- At each age and stage, be mindful about ear infections. Make sure children are hearing properly so they can detect changes in sound patterns.

- Continue reading books with rhyme, rhythm, and repetition at every age.

Resource

Shaywitz, Sally. 2005. *Overcoming Dyslexia: A New and Complete Science-Based Program for Reading Problems at Any Level.* New York: Vintage.

⚡ 52. Use a visual when you first introduce a new idea.

How will knowing this help me?

As you learned in Brain Basics 101, the visual system in the brain is the first to come fully online. The brain uses visual input during the first six months of life to connect neurons rapidly. By the time a baby is six months old, her vision is well established and even depth perception has been achieved. Because this area wires so quickly, much of what a young child learns results from visual input. Even in adults, a large percentage of the brain is devoted to the processing of visual information.

When a human brain learns anything, immediate and continuing physical changes occur, and these changes last. Such is the power of the first learning!

Memory for visual experiences is very strong, in part because it is the first way a child receives information. Visual memory serves as a template for organizing additional information a child learns. Also, psychologists have known for a long time that the brain gives preference to the first and last items in a list or group that a person sees or hears. People tend to forget the items in the middle. So if you want a child to remember something, use visuals and make sure that the most important things come first or last.

So what should I try to do?

- Provide pictures or real objects for new things you want a child to learn.

- Provide picture cues for routines you want a child to learn.

- Use pictures or real objects to gain the child's initial interest in a topic or idea.

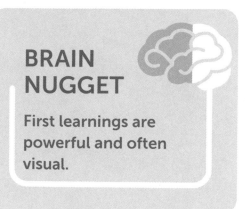

BRAIN NUGGET

First learnings are powerful and often visual.

- Have children draw pictures of the story they are telling. Take dictation to help them label the picture and the story.

- Post important visuals in sequence as reminders of information they have learned. This strategy is especially helpful when you want a child to remember what happened first, next, and last in a story.

EPILOGUE

My purpose in writing this book has been to help the thousands of caregivers who work with children every day and who are doing the very best job they know how to do. I am hoping you will see with different perspectives and learn about ideas recently discovered or confirmed by scientists about how best to stimulate and protect a young child's developing mind.

If you are caring for a young child from birth through age five, you have a tremendous responsibility. You are helping to actually form the brains of children in your care! That can be a daunting idea. It can also be an exhilarating thought. You have the opportunity to really change people's lives for the better. You are stepping up when perhaps few understand your commitment and your sacrifice. You are giving your time and effort to learning everything you can so that the environments you create, the relationships that you form, and the contributions that you make will matter.

Oprah Winfrey said that what she has learned from interviewing thousands of people is that the number-one need that we all have is to know that we matter. Rich or poor, famous or not, we want to know that we are heard and that what we think matters.

Working with infants, toddlers, and preschoolers matters! The United States is facing the stark reality that many, many nations are doing a much better job of caring for children, and it is starting to show up in our ever-sinking ratings on many measures of children's well-being and educational achievement. To turn this around, we will need to make better, tangible investments in children and families. We will need to implement what the scientists now clearly know about how to stimulate and protect a child's brain. I hope that what you have learned in this book will help you in that important mission.

Index

A
accommodation, 78
affect, 99
agency, sense of, 88, 117
alerting, 51, 53, 60, 103
American Academy of Pediatrics, 50, 55, 56
American Psychological Association, 95
amygdala, 12–13
arousal, 53
articulating speech sounds, 105–106
assimilation, 78
attachment, 17
attention
   joint, 119
   tips, 47–66
axons, 26

B
baby talk, 103
bilingualism, encouraging, 80–83
bonding, 17
   tips, 67–97
Boroson, M., 96
brain
   characteristics of all, 14–16
   components of, 8, 10–11
   physical changes, 26–27
   structure and function, 12–14
   timing and influence, 11, 17
brain development
   description of, 7–16
   sequence of, 8–10, 22–26
brain stem, 8, 10
buckets, use of safety, 50–52
Buckleitner, W., 88
Burns, M., 9–10

C
cause-and-effect learning, 15–16
cerebellum, 12
classroom environments, creating soothing, 60–61
code switching, 82
colors, use of bold, 112–113
communication tips, 99–127
connections
   linking new ideas with prior, 30–31
   practice and making, 21–22
continuity of care, 68
corpus callosum, 12
cortex, 10–11
Crane, J., 71
crawling, 36–37

D
dendrites, 26
Developing Mind, The (Siegel), 76
DNA, 37–38
dopamine, 53
dual-language development, encouraging, 80–83
Dweck, C., 87

E
early childhood development, economic benefits of, 40–41
economic benefits of early childhood development, 40–41
emotions, use of, 47–48
enthusiasm, importance of using, 58–59
epigenetics, 38
executive functions, 41, 64–66
eye contact, 59

F

face time, 57–58
facial expressions, 99–100
feedback, providing, 86–87
Field, T., 71
figure-ground discrimination, 112
Fred Rogers Center for Early Learning
    and Children's Media, 88

G

gene expression, 38, 71
Genesee, F., 81
gestures, 48, 107, 109–110, 114
Grunewald, R., 41

H

Hart, B., 101
hearing, 9, 23, 105, 107, 126
Heckman, J., 40
hemispheres
    midline activities, 36–37, 48–49
    right versus left, 9–10, 12, 36, 49
hippocampus, 13, 28
holding, importance of, 52, 72–74
hypothalamus, 12–14

I

imitation, 57–58, 113–115
impulse control, 4, 61–64, 116
infant needs, responding to, 69–71

J

Jha, A., 94
joint attention, 119

K

Kabat-Zinn, J., 94
knowledge,
    linking new ideas with prior, 5, 18–19,
    22, 30–31, 78

L

learning principles, 18–19
limbic system, 8–13, 17, 23, 25, 69, 75
love
    importance of, 4, 10, 15, 17, 29, 40, 67–
    68, 92
    need to express, 75–76

M

maintaining, 51
massage, benefits of gentle, 71–73
meditation, 93–94, 96
midline activities, 36–37, 48–49
mindfulness, 3–4, 27, 93–96
mind-set, 87
mirror neurons, 114–115
motor development, 9, 23, 37, 109, 111, 116
multitasking, 95
music, bonding and use of, 83–86
musical instruments, playing, 110–112, 122
myelin, 27, 44, 118

N

National Association for the Education of
    Young Children, 88
neocortex, 8, 11, 23–24
neural pruning, 21–22
neurons, 7, 11, 19, 26–27, 30, 126
    mirror, 114–115
New Directions Institute for Brain
    Development, 5
novel experiences, role of, 14, 42–43

O

orienting, 51, 60
Overcoming Dyslexia (Shaywitz), 124
overstimulation, avoiding, 60–61

P

parentese, 55, 103–104
pattern recognition, 14–15, 31–34, 53, 54,
    66, 84